PENGUIN BOOKS

The Beauties

1. *Voices of Akenfield* Ronald Blythe
2. *The Wood* John Stewart Collis
3. *From Dover to the Wen* William Cobbett
4. *The Pleasures of English Food* Alan Davidson
5. *Through England on a Side-Saddle* Celia Fiennes
6. *Elegy Written in a Country Churchyard and Other Poems* Various
7. *A Shropshire Lad* A. E. Housman
8. *Cathedrals and Castles* Henry James
9. *Walks in the Wheat-fields* Richard Jefferies
10. *The Beauties of a Cottage Garden* Gertrude Jekyll
11. *Country Churches* Simon Jenkins
12. *A Wiltshire Diary* Francis Kilvert
13. *Some Country Houses and their Owners* James Lees-Milne
14. *The Clouded Mirror* L. T. C. Rolt
15. *Let Us Now Praise Famous Gardens* Vita Sackville-West
16. *One Green Field* Edward Thomas
17. *English Folk Songs* Ralph Vaughan Williams and A. L. Lloyd
18. *Country Lore and Legends* Jennifer Westwood and Jacqueline Simpson
19. *Birds of Selborne* Gilbert White
20. *Life at Grasmere* Dorothy and William Wordsworth

THE
BEAUTIES
OF A
COTTAGE
GARDEN

*Gertrude
Jekyll*

English Journeys

PENGUIN BOOKS

Published by the Penguin Group
Penguin Books Ltd, 80 Strand, London WC2R ORL, England
Penguin Group (USA) Inc., 375 Hudson Street, New York, New York 10014, USA
Penguin Group (Canada), 90 Eglinton Avenue East, Suite 700, Toronto, Ontario, Canada M4P 2Y3
(a division of Pearson Penguin Canada Inc.)
Penguin Ireland, 25 St Stephen's Green, Dublin 2, Ireland
(a division of Penguin Books Ltd)
Penguin Group (Australia), 250 Camberwell Road, Camberwell, Victoria 3124, Australia
(a division of Pearson Australia Group Pty Ltd)
Penguin Books India Pvt Ltd, 11 Community Centre, Panchsheel Park, New Delhi – 110 017, India
Penguin Group (NZ), 67 Apollo Drive, Rosedale, North Shore 0632, New Zealand
(a division of Pearson New Zealand Ltd)
Penguin Books (South Africa) (Pty) Ltd, 24 Sturdee Avenue, Rosebank, Johannesburg 2196, South Africa

Penguin Books Ltd, Registered Offices: 80 Strand, London WC2R ORL, England

www.penguin.com

This selection is taken from *Wood and Garden*, first published in 1899
Published in Penguin Books 2009
3

Set by Rowland Phototypesetting Ltd, Bury St Edmunds, Suffolk
Printed in England by Clays Ltd, St Ives plc

978–0–141–19087–7

www.greenpenguin.co.uk

Penguin Books is committed to a sustainable future
for our business, our readers and our planet.
The book in your hands is made from paper
certified by the Forest Stewardship Council.

Contents

Introductory

There are already many and excellent books about gardening; but the love of a garden, already so deeply implanted in the English heart, is so rapidly growing, that no excuse is needed for putting forth another.

I lay no claim either to literary ability, or to botanical knowledge, or even to knowing the best practical methods of cultivation; but I have lived among outdoor flowers for many years, and have not spared myself in the way of actual labour, and have come to be on closely intimate and friendly terms with a great many growing things, and have acquired certain instincts which, though not clearly defined, are of the nature of useful knowledge.

But the lesson I have thoroughly learnt, and wish to pass on to others, is to know the enduring happiness that the love of a garden gives. I rejoice when I see any one, and especially children, inquiring about flowers, and wanting gardens of their own, and carefully working in them. For the love of gardening is a seed that once sown never dies, but always grows and grows to an enduring and ever-increasing source of happiness.

If in the following chapters I have laid special stress upon gardening for beautiful effect, it is because it is the way of gardening that I love best, and know most about, and that seems to me capable of giving the greatest amount of pleasure. I am strongly for treating garden and wooded ground in a pictorial way, mainly with large effects, and in the second place with lesser beautiful incidents, and for so arranging plants and trees and grassy spaces that they look happy and at home, and make no parade of conscious effort. I try for beauty and harmony everywhere, and especially for harmony of colour. A garden so treated gives the delightful feeling of repose, and refreshment, and purest enjoyment of beauty, that seems to my understanding to be the best fulfilment of its purpose; while to the diligent worker its happiness is like the offering of a constant hymn of praise. For I hold that the best purpose of a garden is to give delight and to give refreshment of mind, to soothe, to refine, and to lift up the heart in a spirit of praise and thankfulness. It is certain that those who practise gardening in the best ways find it to be so.

But the scope of practical gardening covers a range of horticultural practice wide enough to give play to every variety of human taste. Some find their greatest pleasure in collecting as large a number as possible of all sorts of plants from all sources, others in collecting them themselves in their foreign homes, others in making rock-gardens, or ferneries, or peat-gardens, or bog-gardens, or gardens for conifers or for flowering shrubs, or special gardens of plants and trees with variegated or coloured leaves, or in the cultivation of some particular race or family of plants. Others may best like wide lawns with large trees, or wild gardening, or a quite formal garden, with trim hedge and walk, and terrace, and brilliant parterre, or a combination of several ways of gardening. And all are right and reasonable and enjoyable to their owners, and in some way or degree helpful to others.

The way that seems to me most desirable is again different, and I have made an attempt to describe it in some of its aspects. But I have learned much, and am always learning, from other people's gardens, and the lesson I have learned most thoroughly is, never to say 'I know' – there is so infinitely much to learn, and the conditions of different gardens vary so greatly, even when soil and situation appear to be alike and they are in the same district. Nature is such a subtle chemist that one never knows what she is about, or what surprises she may have in store for us.

Often one sees in the gardening papers discussions about the treatment of some particular plant. One man writes to say it can only be done one way, another to say it can only be done quite some other way, and the discussion waxes hot and almost angry, and the puzzled reader, perhaps as yet young in gardening, cannot tell what to make of it. And yet the two writers are both able gardeners, and both absolutely trustworthy, only they should have said, 'In my experience *in this place* such a plant can only be done in such a way.' Even plants of the same family will not do equally well in the same garden. Every practical gardener knows this in the case of strawberries and potatoes; he has to find out which kinds will do in his garden; the experience of his friend in the next county is probably of no use whatever.

I have learnt much from the little cottage gardens that help to make our English waysides the prettiest in the temperate world. One can hardly go into the smallest cottage garden without learning or observing something new. It may be some two plants growing beautifully together by some happy chance, or a pretty mixed tangle of creepers, or something that one always thought must have a south wall doing better on an east one. But eye and brain must be alert to receive the impression and studious to store it, to add to the hoard of experience. And it is important to train oneself to have a good flower-eye; to be able to see at a glance what flowers are good and which are unworthy, and why, and to keep an open mind about it; not to be swayed by the petty tyrannies of the 'florist' or show judge; for, though some part of his judgment may be sound, he is himself a slave to rules, and must go by points which are defined arbitrarily and rigidly, and have reference mainly to the show-table, leaving out of account, as if unworthy of consideration, such matters as gardens and garden beauty, and human delight, and sunshine, and varying lights of morning and evening and noonday. But many, both nurserymen and private people, devote themselves to growing and improving the best classes of hardy flowers, and we can hardly offer them too much grateful praise, or do them too much honour. For what would our gardens be without the Roses, Pæonies, and Gladiolus of France, and the Tulips and Hyacinths of Holland, to say nothing of the hosts of good things raised by our home growers, and of the enterprise of the great firms whose agents are always searching the world for garden treasures?

Let no one be discouraged by the thought of how much there is to learn. Looking back upon nearly thirty years of gardening (the earlier part of it in groping ignorance with scant means of help), I can remember no part of it that was not full of pleasure and encouragement. For the first steps are steps into a delightful Unknown, the first successes are victories all the happier for being scarcely expected, and with the growing knowledge comes the widening outlook, and the comforting sense of an ever-increasing gain of critical appreciation. Each new step becomes a little surer, and each new grasp a little firmer, till, little by little, comes the power of intelligent combination, the nearest thing we can know to the mighty force of creation.

And a garden is a grand teacher. It teaches patience and careful watchfulness; it teaches industry and thrift; above all, it teaches entire trust. 'Paul planteth and Apollo watereth, but God giveth the increase.' The good gardener knows with absolute certainty that if he does his part, if he gives the labour, the love, and every aid that his knowledge of his craft, experience of the conditions of his place, and exercise of his personal wit can work together to suggest, that so surely as he does this diligently and faithfully, so surely will God give the increase. Then with the honestly-earned success comes the consciousness of encouragement to renewed effort, and, as it were, an echo of the gracious words, 'Well done, good and faithful servant.'

1. *Large and Small Gardens*

The size of a garden has very little to do with its merit. It is merely an accident relating to the circumstances of the owner. It is the size of his heart and brain and goodwill that will make his garden either delightful or dull, as the case may be, and either leave it at the usual monotonous dead-level, or raise it, in whatever degree may be, towards that of a work of fine art. If a man knows much, it is more difficult for him to deal with a small space than a larger, for he will have to make the more sacrifice; but if he is wise he will at once make up his mind about what he will let go, and how he may best treat the restricted space. Some years ago I visited a small garden attached to a villa on the outskirts of a watering-place on the south coast. In ordinary hands it would have been a perfectly commonplace thing, with the usual weary mixture, and exhibiting the usual distressing symptoms that come in the train of the ministrations of the jobbing-gardener. In size it may have been a third of an acre, and it was one of the most interesting and enjoyable gardens I have ever seen, its master and mistress giving it daily care and devotion, and enjoying to the full its glad response of grateful growth. The master had built with his own hands, on one side where more privacy was wanted, high rugged walls, with spaces for many rock-loving plants, and had made the wall die away so cleverly into the rock-garden, that the whole thing looked like a garden founded on some ancient ruined structure. And it was all done with so much taste that there was nothing jarring or strained-looking, still less anything cockneyfied, but all easy and pleasant and pretty, while the happy look of the plants at once proclaimed his sympathy with them, and his comprehensive knowledge of their wants. In the same garden was a walled enclosure where Tree Pæonies and some of the hardier of the oriental Rhododendrons were thriving, and there were pretty spaces of lawn, and flower border, and shrub clump, alike beautiful and enjoyable, all within a small space, and yet not crowded – the garden of one who was a keen flower lover, as well as a world-known botanist.

I am always thankful to have seen this garden, because it showed me, in a way that had never been so clearly brought home to me, how much may be done in a small space.

Another and much smaller garden that I remember with pleasure was in a sort of yard among houses, in a country town. The house it belonged to, a rather high one, was on its east side, and halfway along on the south; the rest was bounded by a wall about ten feet high. Opposite the house the owner had built of rough blocks of sandstone what served as a workshop, about twelve feet long along the wall, and six feet wide within. A low archway of the same rough stone was the entrance, and immediately above it a lean-to roof sloped up to the top of the wall, which just here had been carried a little higher. The roof was of large flat sandstones, only slightly lapping over each other, with spaces and chinks where grew luxuriant masses of Polypody Fern. It was contrived with a cement bed, so that it was quite weather-tight, and the room was lighted by a skylight at one end that did not show from the garden. A small surface of lead-flat, on a level with the top of the wall, in one of the opposite angles, carried an old oil-jar, from which fell masses of gorgeous Tropæolum, and the actual surface of the flat was a garden of Stonecrops. The rounded coping of the walls, and the joints in many places (for the wall was an old one), were gay with yellow Corydalis and Snap-dragons and more Stonecrops. The little garden had a few pleasant flowering bushes, Ribes and Laurustinus, a Bay and an Almond tree. In the coolest and shadiest corner were a fern-grotto and a tiny tank. The rest of the garden, only a few yards across, was laid out with a square bed in the middle, and a little path round, then a three-feet-wide border next the wall, all edged with rather tall-grown Box. The middle bed had garden Roses and Carnations, and Mignonette and Stocks. All round were well-chosen plants and shrubs, looking well and happy, though in a confined and rather airless space. Every square foot had been made the most of with the utmost ingenuity, but the ingenuity was always directed by good taste, so that nothing looked crowded or out of place.

And I think of two other gardens of restricted space, both long strips of ground walled at the sides, whose owners I am thankful to count among my friends – one in the favoured climate of the Isle of Wight, a little garden where I suppose there are more rare and beautiful plants brought together within a small space than perhaps in any other garden of the same size in England; the other in a cathedral town, now a memory only, for the master of what was one of the most beautiful gardens I have ever seen now lives elsewhere. The garden was long in shape, and divided about midway by a wall. The division next the house was a quiet lawn, with a mulberry tree and a few mounded borders near the sides that were unobstrusive, and in no way spoilt the quiet feeling of the lawn space. Then a doorway in the dividing wall led to a straight path with a double flower border. I suppose there was a vegetable garden behind the borders, but of that I have no recollection, only a vivid remembrance of that brilliantly beautiful mass of flowers. The picture was good enough as one went along, especially as at the end one came first within sound and then within sight of a rushing river, one of those swift, clear, shallow streams with stony bottom that the trout love; but it was ten times more beautiful on turning to go back, for there was the mass of flowers, and towering high above it the noble mass of the giant structure – one of the greatest and yet most graceful buildings that has ever been raised by man to the glory of God.

It is true that it is not every one that has the advantage of a garden bounded by a river and a noble church, but even these advantages might have been lost by vulgar or unsuitable treatment of the garden. But the mind of the master was so entirely in sympathy with the place, that no one that had the privilege of seeing it could feel that it was otherwise than right and beautiful.

Both these were the gardens of clergymen; indeed, some of our greatest gardeners are, and have been, within the ranks of the Church. For have we not a brilliantly-gifted dignitary whose loving praise of the Queen of flowers has become a classic? and have we not among churchmen the greatest grower of seedling Daffodils the world has yet seen, and other names of clergymen honourably associated with Roses and Auriculas and Tulips and other good flowers, and all greatly to their bettering? The conditions of the life of a parish priest would tend to make him a good gardener, for, while other men roam about, he stays mostly at home, and to live with one's garden is one of the best ways to ensure its welfare. And then, among the many anxieties and vexations and disappointments that must needs grieve the heart of the pastor of his people, his garden, with its wholesome labour and all its lessons of patience and trust and hopefulness, and its comforting power of solace, must be one of the best of medicines for the healing of his often sorrowing soul.

I do not envy the owners of very large gardens. The garden should fit its master or his tastes just as his clothes do; it should be neither too large nor too small, but just comfortable. If the garden is larger than he can individually govern and plan and look after, then he is no longer its master but its slave, just as surely as the much-too-rich man is the slave and not the master of his superfluous wealth. And when I hear of the great place with a kitchen garden of twenty acres within the walls,

my heart sinks as I think of the uncomfortable dispro-
portion between the man and those immediately around
him, and his vast output of edible vegetation, and I fall
to wondering how much of it goes as it should go, or
whether the greater part of it does not go dribbling
away, leaking into unholy back-channels; and of how
the looking after it must needs be subdivided; and of
how many side-interests are likely to steal in, and altogether how great a burden of anxiety or matter of
temptation it must give rise to. A grand truth is in the
old farmer's saying, 'The master's eye makes the pig fat;'
but how can any one master's eye fat that vast pig of
twenty acres, with all its minute and costly cultivation,
its two or three crops a year off all ground given to soft
vegetables, its stoves, greenhouses, orchid and orchard
houses, its vineries, pineries, figgeries, and all manner of
glass structures?

But happily these monstrous gardens are but few – I
only know of or have seen two, and I hope never to see
another.

Nothing is more satisfactory than to see the well-
designed and well-organised garden of the large country
house, whose master loves his garden, and has good
taste and a reasonable amount of leisure.

I think that the first thing in such a place is to have
large unbroken lawn spaces – all the better if they are
continuous, passing round the south and west sides of
the house. I am supposing a house of the best class, but
not necessarily of the largest size. Immediately adjoining
the house, except for the few feet needed for a border
for climbing plants, is a broad walk, dry and smooth, and

perfectly level from end to end. This, in the case of many houses, and nearly always with good effect, is raised two or three feet above the garden ground, and if the architecture of the house demands it, has a retaining wall surmounted by a balustrade of masonry and wrought stone. Broad and shallow stone steps lead down to the turf both at the end of the walk and in the middle of the front of the house, the wider and shallower the better, and at the foot of the wall may be a narrow border for a few climbing plants that will here and there rise above the coping of the parapet. I do not think it desirable where there are stone balusters or other distinct architectural features to let them be smothered with climbing plants, but that there should be, say, a *Pyrus japonica* or an Escallonia, and perhaps a white Jasmine, and on a larger space perhaps a cut-leaved or a Claret Vine. Some of the best effects of the kind I have seen were where the bush, being well established, rose straight out of the grass, the border being unnecessary except just at the beginning.

The large lawn space I am supposing stretches away a good distance from the house, and is bounded on the south and west by fine trees; away beyond that is all wild wood. On summer afternoons the greater part of the lawn expanse is in cool shade, while winter sunsets show through the tree stems. Towards the south-east the wood would pass into shrub plantations, and farther still into garden and wild orchard (of which I shall have something to say presently). At this end of the lawn would be the brilliant parterre of bedded plants, seen both from the shaded lawn and from the terrace, which at this end forms part of its design. Beyond the parterre would be a distinct division from the farther garden, either of Yew or Box hedge, with bays for seats, or in the case of a change of level, of another terrace wall. The next space beyond would be the main garden for hardy plants, at its southern end leading into the wild orchard. This would be the place for the free garden or the reserve garden, or for any of the many delightful ways in which hardy flowers can be used; and if it happened by good fortune to have a stream or any means of having running water, the possibilities of beautiful gardening would be endless.

Beyond this again would come the kitchen garden, and after that the stables and the home farm. If the kitchen garden had a high wall, and might be entered on this side by handsome wrought-iron gates, I would approach it from the parterre by a broad grass walk bounded by large Bay trees at equal intervals to right and left. Through these to the right would be seen the free garden of hardy flowers.

For the kitchen garden a space of two acres would serve a large country house with all that is usually grown within walls, but there should always be a good space outside for the rougher vegetables, as well as a roomy yard for compost, pits and frames, and rubbish.

And here I wish to plead on behalf of the gardener that he should have all reasonable comforts and conveniences. Nothing is more frequent, even in good places, than to find the potting and tool sheds screwed away into some awkward corner, badly lighted, much too small, and altogether inadequate, and the pits and frames scattered about and difficult to get at. Nothing is more wasteful of time, labour, or temper. The working parts of a large garden form a complicated organisation, and if the parts of the mechanism do not fit and work well, and are not properly eased and oiled, still more, if any are missing, there must be disastrous friction and damage and loss of power. In designing garden buildings, I always strongly urge in connection with the heating system a warmed potting shed and a comfortable mess-room for the men, and over this a perfectly dry loft for drying and storing such matters as shading material, nets, mats, ropes, and sacks. If this can be warmed, so much the better. There must also be a convenient and quite frost-proof place for winter storing of vegetable roots and such plants as Dahlias, Cannas, and Gladiolus; and also a well-lighted and warmed workshop for all the innumerable jobs put aside for wet weather, of which the chief will be repainting and glazing of lights, repairing implements, and grinding and setting tools. This shop should have a carpenter's bench and screw, and a smith's anvil, and a proper assortment of tools. Such arrangements, well planned and thought out, will save much time and loss of produce, besides helping to make all the people employed more comfortable and happy.

I think that a garden should never be large enough to be tiring, that if a large space has to be dealt with, a great part had better be laid out in wood. Woodland is always charming and restful and enduringly beautiful, and then there is an intermediate kind of woodland that should be made more of – woodland of the orchard type. Why is the orchard put out of the way, as it generally is, in some remote region beyond the kitchen garden and stables? I should like the lawn, or the hardy flower garden, or both, to pass directly into it on one side, and to plant a space of several acres, not necessarily in the usual way, with orchard standards twenty-five feet apart in straight rows (though in many places the straight rows might be best), but to have groups and even groves of such things as Medlars and Quinces, Siberian and Chinese Crabs, Damsons, Prunes, Service trees, and Mountain Ash, besides Apples, Pears, and Cherries, in both standard and bush forms. Then alleys of Filbert and Cob-nut, and in the opener spaces tangles or brakes of the many beautiful bushy things allied to the Apple and Plum tribe – *Cydonia* and *Prunus triloba* and *Cratægus* of many kinds (some of them are tall bushes or small trees with beautiful fruits); and the wild Blackthorn, which, though a plum, is so nearly related to pear that pears may be grafted on it. And then brakes of Blackberries, especially of the Parsley-leaved kind, so free of growth and so generous of fruit. How is it that this fine native plant is almost invariably sold in nurseries as an American bramble? If I am mistaken in this I should be glad to be corrected, but I believe it to be only the cut-leaved variety of the native *Rubus affinis*.

I have tried the best of the American kinds, and with the exception of one year, when I had a few fine fruits from Kittatinny, they had been a failure, whereas invariably when people have told me that their American Blackberries have fruited well, I have found them to be the Parsley-leaved.

Some members of the large Rose-Apple-Plum tribe grow to be large forest trees, and in my wild orchard they would go in the farther parts. The Bird-cherry (*Prunus padus*) grows into a tree of the largest size. A Mountain Ash will sometimes have a trunk two feet in diameter, and a head of a size to suit. The American kind, its near relation, but with larger leaves and still grander masses of berries, is a noble small tree; and the native white Beam should not be forgotten, and choice places should be given to Amelanchier and the lovely double Japan Apple (*Pyrus Malus floribunda*). To give due space and effect to all these good things my orchard garden would run into a good many acres, but every year it would be growing into beauty and profit. The grass should be left rough, and plentifully planted with Daffodils, and with Cowslips if the soil is strong. The grass would be mown and made into hay in June, and perhaps mown once more towards the end of September. Under the nut-trees would be Primroses and the garden kinds of wood Hyacinths and Dogtooth Violets and Lily of the Valley, and perhaps Snowdrops, or any of the smaller bulbs that most commended themselves to the taste of the master.

Such an orchard garden, well-composed and beautifully grouped, always with that indispensable quality of good 'drawing', would not only be a source of unending pleasure to those who lived in the place, but a valuable lesson to all who saw it; for it would show the value of the simple and sensible ways of using a certain class of related trees and bushes, and of using them with a deliberate intention of making the best of them, instead of the usual meaningless-nohow way of planting. This, in nine cases out of ten, means either ignorance or carelessness, the planter not caring enough about the matter to take the trouble to find out what is best to be done, and being quite satisfied with a mixed lot of shrubs, as offered in nursery sales, or with the choice of the nurseryman. I do not presume to condemn all mixed planting, only stupid and ignorant mixed planting. It is not given to all people to take their pleasures alike; and I have in my mind four gardens, all of the highest interest, in which the planting is all mixed; but then the mixture is of admirable ingredients, collected and placed on account of individual merit, and a ramble round any one of these in company with its owner is a pleasure and a privilege that one cannot prize too highly. Where the garden is of such large extent that experimental plant-ing is made with a good number of one good thing at a time, even though there was no premeditated intention of planting for beautiful effect, the fact of there being enough plants to fall into large groups, and to cover some extent of ground, produces numbers of excellent results. I remember being struck with this on several occasions when I have had the happiness of visiting Mr G. F. Wilson's garden at Wisley, a garden which I take to be about the most instructive it is possible to see. In one part, where the foot of the hill joined the copse, there were hosts of lovely things planted on a succession of rather narrow banks. Almost unthinkingly I expressed the regret I felt that so much individual beauty should be there without an attempt to arrange it for good effect. Mr Wilson stopped, and looking at me straight with a kindly smile, said very quietly, 'That is your business, not mine.' In spite of its being a garden whose first object is trial and experiment, it has left in my memory two pictures, among several lesser ones, of plant-beauty that will stay with me as long as I can remember anything, one an autumn and one a spring picture – the hedge of *Rosa rugosa* in full fruit, and a plantation of *Primula denticulata*. The Primrose was on a bit of level ground, just at the outer and inner edges of the hazel copse. The plants were both grouped and thinly sprinkled, just as nature plants – possibly they grew directly there from seed. They were in superb and luxuriant beauty in the black peaty-looking half-boggy earth, the handsome leaves of the brilliant colour and large size that told of perfect health and vigour, and the large round heads of pure lilac flower carried on strong stalks that must have been fifteen inches high. I never saw it so happy and so beautiful. It is a plant I much admire, and I do the best I can for it on my dry hill; but the conditions of my garden do not allow of any approach to the success of the Wisley plants; still I have treasured that lesson among many others I have brought away from that good garden, and never fail to advise some such treatment when I see the likely home for it in other places.

Some of the most delightful of all gardens are the little strips in front of roadside cottages. They have a simple and tender charm that one may look for in vain in gardens of greater pretension. And the old garden flowers seem to know that there they are seen at their best; for where else can one see such Wallflowers, or Double Daisies, or White Rose bushes; such clustering masses of perennial Peas, or such well-kept flowery edgings of Pink, or Thrift, or London Pride?

Among a good many calls for advice about laying out gardens, I remember an early one that was of special interest. It was the window-box of a factory lad in one of the great northern manufacturing towns. He had advertised in a mechanical paper that he wanted a tiny garden, as full of interest as might be, in a window-box; he knew nothing – would somebody help him with advice? So advice was sent and the box prepared. If I remember rightly the size was three feet by ten inches. A little later the post brought him little plants of mossy and silvery saxifrages, and a few small bulbs. Even some stones were sent, for it was to be a rock-garden, and there were to be two hills of different heights with rocky tops, and a longish valley with a sunny and a shady side.

It was delightful to have the boy's letters, full of keen interest and eager questions, and only difficult to restrain him from killing his plants with kindness, in the way of liberal doses of artificial manure. The very smallness of the tiny garden made each of its small features the more precious. I could picture his feeling of delightful anticipation when he saw the first little bluish blade of the Snowdrop patch pierce its mossy carpet. Would it, could it really grow into a real Snowdrop, with the modest, milk-white flower and the pretty green hearts on the outside of the inner petals, and the clear green stripes within? and would it really nod him a glad good-morning when he opened his window to greet it? And those few blunt reddish horny-looking snouts just coming through the ground, would they really grow into the brilliant blue of the early Squill, that would be like a bit of midsummer sky among the grimy surroundings of the attic window, and under that grey, soot-laden northern sky? I thought with pleasure how he would watch them in spare minutes of the dinner-hour spent at home, and think of them as he went forward and back to his work, and how the remembrance of the tender beauty of the full-blown flower would make him glad, and lift up his heart while 'minding his mule' in the busy restless mill.

2. Beginning and Learning

Many people who love flowers and wish to do some practical gardening are at their wits' end to know what to do and how to begin. Like a person who is on skates for the first time, they feel that, what with the bright steel runners, and the slippery surface, and the sense of helplessness, there are more ways of tumbling about than of progressing safely in any one direction. And in gardening the beginner must feel this kind of perplexity and helplessness, and indeed there is a great deal to learn, only it is pleasant instead of perilous, and the many tumbles by the way only teach and do not hurt. The first few steps are perhaps the most difficult, and it is only when we know something of the subject and an eager beginner comes with questions that one sees how very many are the things that want knowing. And the more ignorant the questioner, the more difficult it is to answer helpfully. When one knows, one cannot help presupposing some sort of knowledge on the part of the querist, and where this is absent the answer we can give is of no use. The ignorance, when fairly complete, is of such a nature that the questioner does not know what to ask, and the answer, even if it can be given, falls upon barren ground. I think in such cases it is better to try and teach one simple thing at a time, and not to attempt to answer a number of useless questions. It is disheartening when one has tried to give a careful answer to have it received with an Oh! of boredom or disappointment, as much as to say, You can't expect me to take all that trouble; and there is the still more unsatisfactory sort of applicant, who plies a string of questions and will not wait for the answers! The real way is to try and learn a little from everybody and from every place. There is no royal road. It is no use asking me or any one else how to dig – I mean sitting indoors and asking it. Better go and watch a man digging, and then take a spade and try to do it, and go on trying till it comes, and you gain the knack that is to be learnt with all tools, of doubling the power and halving the effort; and meanwhile you will be learning other things, about your own arms and legs and back, and perhaps a little robin will come and give you moral support, and at the same time keep a sharp look-out for any worms you may happen to turn up; and you will find out that there are all sorts of ways of learning, not only from people and books, but from sheer trying.

I remember years ago having to learn to use the blow-pipe, for soldering and other purposes connected with work in gold and silver. The difficult part of it is to keep up the stream of air through the pipe while you are breathing the air in; it is easy enough when you only want a short blast of a few seconds, within the compass of one breath or one filling of the bellows (lungs), but often one has to go on blowing through several inspirations. It is a trick of muscular action. My master who taught me never could do it himself, but by much trying one day I caught the trick.

The grand way to learn, in gardening as in all things else, is to wish to learn, and to be determined to find out – not to think that any one person can wave a wand and give the power and knowledge. And there will be plenty of mistakes, and there must be, just as children must pass through the usual childish complaints. And some people make the mistake of trying to begin at the end, and of using recklessly what may want the utmost caution, such, for instance, as strong chemical manures.

Some ladies asked me why their plant had died. They had got it from the very best place, and they were sure they had done their very best for it, and – there it was, dead. I asked what it was, and how they had treated it. It was some ordinary border plant, whose identity I now forget; they had made a nice hole with their new trowel, and for its sole benefit they had bought a tin of Concentrated Fertiliser. This they had emptied into the hole, put in the plant, and covered it up and given it lots of water, and – it had died! And yet these were the best and kindest of women, who would never have dreamed of feeding a new-born infant on beefsteaks and raw brandy. But they learned their lesson well, and at once saw the sense when I pointed out that a plant with naked roots just taken out of the ground or a pot, removed from one feeding-place and not yet at home in another, or still more after a journey, with the roots only wrapped in a little damp moss and paper, had its feeding power suspended for a time, and was in the position of a helpless invalid. All that could be done for it then was a little bland nutriment of weak slops and careful nursing; if the planting took place in the summer it would want shading and only very gentle watering, until firm root-hold was secured and root-appetite became active, and that in rich and well-prepared garden ground such as theirs strong artificial manure was in any case superfluous.

When the earlier ignorances are overcome it becomes much easier to help and advise, because there is more common ground to stand on. In my own case, from quite a small child, I had always seen gardening going on, though not of a very interesting kind. Nothing much was thought of but bedding plants, and there was a rather large space on each side of the house for these, one on gravel and one on turf. But I had my own little garden in a nook beyond the shrubbery, with a seat shaded by a *Boursault elegans* Rose, which I thought then, and still think, one of the loveliest of its kind. But my first knowledge of garden plants came through wild ones. Some one gave me that excellent book, the Rev. C. A. Johns' 'Flowers of the Field.' For many years I had no one to advise me (I was still quite small) how to use the book, or how to get to know (though it stared me in the face) how the plants were in large related families, and I had not the sense to do it for myself, nor to learn the introductory botanical part, which would have saved much trouble afterwards; but when I brought home my flowers I would take them one by one and just turn over the pages till I came to the picture that looked something like. But in this way I got a knowledge of individuals, and afterwards the idea of broad classification and relationship of genera to species may have come all the easier. I always think of that book as the most precious gift I ever received. I distinctly trace to its teaching my first firm steps in the path of plant knowledge, and the feeling of assured comfort I had afterwards in recognising the kinds when I came to collect garden plants; for at that time I had no other garden book, no means of access to botanic gardens or private collections, and no helpful adviser. One copy of 'Johns' I wore right out; I have now two, of which one is in its second binding, and is always near me for reference. I need hardly say that this was long before the days of the 'English Flower-Garden,' or its helpful predecessor, 'Alpine Plants.'

By this time I was steadily collecting hardy garden plants wherever I could find them, mostly from cottage gardens. Many of them were still unknown to me by name, but as the collection increased I began to compare and discriminate, and of various kinds of one plant to throw out the worse and retain the better, and to train myself to see what made a good garden plant, and about then began to grow the large yellow and white bunch Primroses, whose history is in another chapter. And then I learnt that there were such places (though then but few) as nurseries, where such plants as I had been collecting in the cottage gardens, and even better, were grown. And I went to Osborne's at Fulham (now all built over), and there saw the original tree of the fine Ilex known as the Fulham Oak, and several spring-flowering bulbs I had never seen before, and what I felt sure were numbers of desirable summer-flowering plants, but not then in bloom. Soon after this I began to learn something about Daffodils, and enjoyed much kind help from Mr Barr, visiting his nursery (then at Tooting) several times, and sometimes combining a visit to Parker's nursery just over the way, a perfect paradise of good hardy plants. I shall never forget my first sight here of the Cape Pondweed (*Aponogeton distachyon*) in full flower and great vigour in the dipping tanks, and overflowing from them into the ditches.

Also I was delighted to see the use as labels of old wheel-spokes. I could not help feeling that if one had been a spoke of a cab-wheel, and had passed all one's working life in being whirled and clattered over London pavements, defiled with street mud, how pleasant a way to end one's days was this; to have one's felloe end pointed and dipped in nice wholesome rot-resisting gas-tar and thrust into the quiet cool earth, and one's nave end smoothed and painted and inscribed with some such soothing legend as *Vinca minor* or *Dianthus fragrans*!

Later I made acquaintance with several of the leading amateur and professional gardeners, and with Mr Robinson, and to their good comradeship and kindly willingness to let me 'pick their brains' I owe a great advance in garden lore. Moreover, what began by the drawing together of a common interest has grown into a still greater benefit, for several acquaintances so made have ripened into steady and much-valued friendships. It has been a great interest to me to have had the privilege of watching the gradual growth, through its several editions, of Mr Robinson's 'English Flower-Garden', the one best and most helpful book of all for those who want to know about hardy flowers; offering as it does in the clearest and easiest way a knowledge of the

garden-treasures of the temperate world. No one who
has not had occasional glimpses behind the scenes can
know how much labour and thought such a book represents, to say nothing of research and practical experiment, and of the trouble and great expense of producing
the large amount of pictorial illustration. Another book,
though on quite different lines, that I find most useful is
Mr Nicholson's 'Illustrated Dictionary of Gardening,' in
eight handy volumes. It covers much the same ground
as the useful old Johnson's 'Gardener's Dictionary,' but
is much more complete and comprehensive, and is copi-
ously illustrated with excellent wood-cuts. It is the work
of a careful and learned botanist, treating of all plants
desirable for cultivation from all climates, and teaching
all branches of practical horticulture and such useful
matters as means of dealing with insect pests. The old
'Johnson' is still a capital book in one volume; mine is
rather out of date, being the edition of 1875, but it has
been lately revised and improved. It would be delightful
to possess, or to have easy access to, a good botanical
library; still, for all the purposes of the average garden
lover, these books will suffice.

I think it is desirable, when a certain degree of knowledge of plants and facility of dealing with them has been
acquired, to get hold of a clear idea of what one most
wishes to do. The scope of the subject is so wide, and
there are so many ways to choose from, that having
one general idea helps one to concentrate thought and
effort that would otherwise be wasted by being diluted
and dribbled through too many probable channels of
waste.

Ever since it came to me to feel some little grasp of knowledge of means and methods, I have found that my greatest pleasure, both in garden and woodland, has been in the enjoyment of beauty of a pictorial kind. Whether the picture be large as of a whole landscape, or of lesser extent as in some fine single group or effect, or within the space of only a few inches as may be seen in some happily-disposed planting of Alpines, the intention is always the same; or whether it is the grouping of trees in the wood by the removal of those whose lines are not wanted in the picture, or in the laying out of broad grassy ways in woody places, or by ever so slight a turn or change of direction in a wood path, or in the alteration of some arrangement of related groups, for form or for massing of light and shade, or for any of the many local conditions that guide one towards forming a decision, the intention is still always the same – to try and make a beautiful garden-picture. And little as I can as yet boast of being able to show anything like the number of these I could wish, yet during the flower-year there is generally something that at least in part answers to the effort.

I do not presume to urge the acceptance of my own particular form of pleasure in a garden on those to whom, from different temperament or manner of education, it would be unwelcome; I only speak of what I feel, and to a certain degree understand; but I had the advantage in earlier life of some amount of training in appreciation of the fine arts, and this, working upon an inborn feeling of reverent devotion to things of the highest beauty in the works of God, has helped me to an understanding of their divinely-inspired interpretations by the noblest minds of men, into those other forms that we know as works of fine art.

And so it comes about that those of us who feel and understand in this way do not exactly attempt to imitate Nature in our gardens, but try to become well acquainted with her moods and ways, and then discriminate in our borrowing, and so interpret her methods as best we may to the making of our garden-pictures.

I have always had great delight in the study of colour, as the word is understood by artists, which again is not a positive matter, but one of relation and proportion. And when one hears the common chatter about 'artistic colours,' one receives an unpleasant impression about the education and good taste of the speaker; and one is reminded of an old saying which treats of the unwisdom of rushing in 'where angels fear to tread,' and of regret that a good word should be degraded by misuse. It may be safely said that no colour can be called artistic in itself; for, in the first place, it is bad English, and in the second, it is nonsense. Even if the first objection were waived, and the second condoned, it could only be used in a secondary sense, as signifying something that is useful and suitable and right in its place. In this limited sense the scarlet of the soldier's coat, and of the pillar-box and mail-cart, and the bright colours of flags, or of the port and starboard lights of ships, might be said to be just so far 'artistic' (again if grammar would allow), as they are right and good in their places. But then those who use the word in the usual ignorant-random way have not even this simple conception of its meaning. Those who know nothing about colour in the more refined sense (and like a knowledge of everything else it wants learning) get no farther than to enjoy it only when most crude and garish – when, as George Herbert says, it 'bids the rash gazer wipe his eye,' or when there is some violent opposition of complementary colour – forgetting, or not knowing, that though in detail the objects brought together may make each other appear brighter, yet in the mass, and especially when mixed up, the one actually neutralises the other. And they have no idea of using the colour of flowers as precious jewels in a setting of quiet environment, or of suiting the colour of flowering groups to that of the neighbouring foliage, thereby enhancing the value of both, or of massing related or harmonious colourings so as to lead up to the most powerful and brilliant effects; and yet all these are just the ways of employing colour to the best advantage.

But the most frequent fault, whether in composition or in colour, is the attempt to crowd too much into the picture; the simpler effect obtained by means of temperate and wise restraint is always the more telling.

3. The Primrose Garden

It must be some five-and-twenty years ago that I began to work at what I may now call my own strain of Primroses, improving it a little every year by careful selection of the best for seed. The parents of the strain were a named kind, called Golden Plover, and a white one, without name, that I found in a cottage garden. I had also a dozen plants about eight or nine years ago from a strong strain of Mr Anthony Waterer's that was running on nearly the same lines; but a year later, when I had flowered them side by side, I liked my own one rather the best, and Mr Waterer, seeing them soon after, approved of them so much that he took some to work with his own. I hold Mr Waterer's strain in great admiration, and, though I tried for a good many years, never could come near him in red colourings. But as my own taste favoured the delicately-shaded flowers, and the ones most liked in the nursery seemed to be those with strongly contrasting eye, it is likely that the two strains may be working still farther apart.

They are, broadly speaking, white and yellow varieties of the strong bunch-flowered or Polyanthus kind, but they vary in detail so much, in form, colour, habit, arrangement, and size of eye and shape of edge, that one year thinking it might be useful to classify them I tried to do so, but gave it up after writing out the characters of sixty classes! Their possible variation seems endless. Every year among the seedlings there appear a number of charming flowers with some new development of size, or colour of flower, or beauty of foliage, and yet all within the narrow bounds of – white and yellow Primroses.

Their time of flowering is much later than that of the true or single-stalked Primrose. They come into bloom early in April, though a certain number of poorly-developed flowers generally come much earlier, and they are at their best in the last two weeks of April and the first days of May. When the bloom wanes, and is nearly overtopped by the leaves, the time has come that I find best for dividing and re-planting. The plants then seem willing to divide, some almost falling apart in one's hands, and the new roots may be seen just beginning to form at the base of the crown. The plants are at the same time relieved of the crowded mass of flower-stem, and, therefore, of the exhausting effort of forming seed, a severe drain on their strength. A certain number will not have made more than one strong crown, and a few single-crown plants have not flowered; these, of course, do not divide. During the flowering time I keep a good look-out for those that I judge to be the most beautiful and desirable, and mark them for seed. These are also taken up, but are kept apart, the flower stems reduced to one or two of the most promising, and they are then planted in a separate place – some cool nursery corner. I find that the lifting and re-planting in no way checks the growth or well-being of the seed-pods.

I remember some years ago a warm discussion in the gardening papers about the right time to sow the seed. Some gardeners of high standing were strongly for sowing it as soon as ripe, while others equally trustworthy advised holding it over till March. I have tried both ways, and have satisfied myself that it is a matter for experiment and decision in individual gardens. As nearly as I can make out, it is well in heavy soils to sow when ripe, and in light ones to wait till March. In some heavy soils Primroses stand well for two years without division; whereas in light ones, such as mine, they take up the food within reach in a much shorter time, so that by the second year the plant has become a crowded mass of weak crowns that only throw up poor flowers, and are by then so much exhausted that they are not worth dividing afterwards. In my own case, having tried both ways, I find the March sown ones much the best.

The seed is sown in boxes in cold frames, and pricked out again into boxes when large enough to handle. The seedlings are planted out in June, when they seem to go on without any check whatever, and are just right for blooming next spring.

The Primrose garden is in a place by itself – a clearing half shaded by Oak, Chestnut, and Hazel. I always think of the Hazel as a kind nurse to Primroses; in the copses they generally grow together, and the finest Primrose plants are often nestled close in to the base of the nut-stool. Three paths run through the Primrose garden, mere narrow tracks between the beds, converging at both ends, something like the lines of longitude on a globe, the ground widening in the middle where there are two good-sized Oaks, and coming to a blunt point at each end, the only other planting near it being two other long-shaped strips of Lily of the Valley.

Every year, before replanting, the Primrose ground is dug over and well manured. All day for two days I sit on a low stool dividing the plants; a certain degree of facility and expertness has come of long practice. The 'rubber' for frequent knife-sharpening is in a pail of water by my side; the lusciously fragrant heap of refuse leaf and flower-stem and old stocky root rises in front of me, changing its shape from a heap to a ridge, as when it comes to a certain height and bulk I back and back away from it. A boy feeds me with armfuls of newly-dug-up plants, two men are digging-in the cooling cow-dung at the farther end, and another carries away the divided plants tray by tray, and carefully replants them. The still air, with only the very gentlest south-westerly breath in it, brings up the mighty boom of the great ship guns from the old seaport, thirty miles away, and the pheasants answer to the sound as they do to thunder. The early summer air is of a perfect temperature, the soft coo of the wood-dove comes down from the near wood, the nightingale sings almost overhead, but – either human happiness may never be quite complete, or else one is not philosophic enough to contemn life's lesser evils, for – oh, the midges!

4. *Colours of Flowers*

I am always surprised at the vague, not to say reckless, fashion in which garden folk set to work to describe the colours of flowers, and at the way in which quite wrong colours are attributed to them. It is done in perfect good faith, and without the least consciousness of describing wrongly. In many cases it appears to be because the names of certain substances have been used conventionally or poetically to convey the idea of certain colours. And some of these errors are so old that they have acquired a kind of respectability, and are in a way accepted without challenge. When they are used about familiar flowers it does not occur to one to detect them, because one knows the flower and its true colour; but when the same old error is used in the description of a new flower, it is distinctly misleading. For instance, when we hear of golden buttercups, we know that it means bright-yellow buttercups; but in the case of a new flower, or one not generally known, surely it is better and more accurate to say bright yellow at once. Nothing is more frequent in plant catalogues than 'bright golden yellow,' when bright yellow is meant. Gold is not bright yellow. I find that a gold piece laid on a gravel path, or against a sandy bank, nearly matches it in colour; and I cannot think of any flower that matches or even approaches the true colour of gold, though something near it may be seen in the pollen-covered anthers of many flowers. A match for gold may more nearly be found among dying beech leaves, and some dark colours of straw or dry grass bents, but none of these when they match the gold are bright yellow. In literature it is quite another matter; when the poet or imaginative writer says, 'a field of golden buttercups,' or 'a golden sunset,' he is quite right, because he appeals to our artistic perception, and in such case only uses the word as an image of something that is rich and sumptuous and glowing.

The same irrelevance of comparison seems to run through all the colours. Flowers of a full, bright-blue colour are often described as of a 'brilliant amethystine blue.' Why amethystine? The amethyst, as we generally see it, is a stone of a washy purple colour, and though there are amethysts of a fine purple, they are not so often seen as the paler ones, and I have never seen one even faintly approaching a really blue colour. What, therefore, is the sense of likening a flower, such as a Delphinium, which is really of a splendid pure-blue colour, to the duller and totally different colour of a third-rate gem?

Another example of the same slip-slop is the term flame-coloured, and it is often preceded by the word 'gorgeous.' This contradictory mixture of terms is generally used to mean bright scarlet. When I look at a flame, whether of fire or candle, I see that the colour is a rather pale yellow, with a reddish tinge about its upper forks, and side wings often of a bluish white – no scarlet anywhere. The nearest approach to red is in the coals, not in the flame. In the case of the candle, the point of the wick is faintly red when compared with the flame, but about the flame there is no red whatever. A distant bonfire looks red at night, but I take it that the apparent redness is from seeing the flames through damp atmosphere, just as the harvest-moon looks red when it rises.

And the strange thing is that in all these cases the likeness to the unlike, and much less bright, colour is given with an air of conferring the highest compliment on the flower in question. It is as if, wishing to praise some flower of a beautiful blue, one called it a brilliant slate-roof blue. This sounds absurd, because it is unfamiliar, but the unsuitability of the comparison is scarcely greater than in the examples just quoted.

It seems most reasonable in describing the colour of flowers to look out for substances whose normal colour shows but little variation – such, for example, as sulphur. The colour of sulphur is nearly always the same. Citron, lemon, and canary are useful colour-names, indicating different strengths of pure pale yellow, inclining towards a tinge of the palest green. Gentian-blue is a useful word, bringing to mind the piercingly powerful hue of the Gentianella. So also is turquoise-blue, for the stone has little variety of shade, and the colour is always of the same type. Forget-me-not blue is also a good word, meaning the colour of the native water Forget-me-not. Sky-blue is a little vague, though it has come by the 'crystallising' force of usage to stand for a blue rather pale than full, and not far from that of the Forget-me-not; indeed, I seem to remember written passages in which the colours of flower and firmament were used reciprocally, the one in describing the other. Cobalt is a word sometimes used, but more often misused, for only water-colour painters know just what it represents, and it is of little use, as it so rarely occurs among flowers.

Crimson is a word to beware of; it covers such a wide extent of ground, and is used so carelessly in plant-catalogues, that one cannot know whether it stands for a rich blood colour or for a malignant magenta. For the latter class of colour the term amaranth, so generally used in French plant-lists, is extremely useful, both as a definition and a warning. Salmon is an excellent colour-word, copper is also useful, the two covering a limited range of beautiful colouring of the utmost value. Blood-red is also accurately descriptive. Terracotta is useful but indefinite, as it may mean anything between brick-red and buff. Red-lead, if it would be accepted as a colour-word, would be useful, denoting the shades of colour between the strongest orange and the palest scarlet, frequent in the lightest of the Oriental Poppies. Amber is a misleading word, for who is to know when it means the transparent amber, whose colour approaches that of resin, or the pale, almost opaque, dull-yellow kind. And what is meant by coral-red? It is the red of the old-fashioned dull-scarlet coral, or of the pink kind more recently in favour?

The terms bronze and smoke may well be used in their place, as in describing or attempting to describe the wonderful colouring of such flowers as Spanish Iris, and the varieties of Iris of the *squalens* section. But often in describing a flower a reference to texture much helps and strengthens the colour-word. I have often described the modest little *Iris tuberosa* as a flower made of green satin and black velvet. The green portion is only slightly green, but is entirely green satin, and the black of the velvet is barely black, but is quite black-velvet-like. The texture of the flower of *Ornithogalum nutans* is silver satin, neither very silvery nor very satin-like, and yet so nearly suggesting the texture of both that the words may well be used in speaking of it. Indeed, texture plays so important a part in the appearance of colour-surface, that one can hardly think of colour without also thinking of texture. A piece of black satin and a piece of black velvet may be woven of the same batch of material, but when the satin is finished and the velvet cut, the appearance is often so dissimilar that they may look quite different in colour. A working painter is never happy if you give him an oil-colour pattern to match in distemper; he must have it of the same texture, or he will not undertake to get it like.

What a wonderful range of colouring there is in black alone to a trained colour-eye! There is the dull brown-black of soot, and the velvety brown-black of the bean-flower's blotch; to my own eye, I have never found anything so entirely black in a natural product as the patch on the lower petals of *Iris iberica*. Is it not Ruskin who says of Velasquez, that there is more colour in his black than in many another painter's whole palette? The blotch of the bean-flower appears black at first, till you look at it close in the sunlight, and then you see its rich velvety texture, so nearly like some of the brown-velvet markings on butterflies' wings. And the same kind of rich colour and texture occurs again on some of the tough

flat half-round funguses, marked with shaded rings, that
grow out of old posts, and that I always enjoy as lessons
of lovely colour-harmony of grey and brown and black.

Much to be regretted is the disuse of the old word
murrey, now only employed in heraldry. It stands for
a dull red-purple, such as appears in the flower of the
Virginian Allspice, and in the native Hound's-tongue,
and often in seedling Auriculas. A fine strong-growing
border Auricula was given to me by my valued friend
the Curator of the Trinity College Botanic Garden,
Dublin, to which he had given the excellently descriptive
name, 'Old Murrey.'

Sage-green is a good colour-word, for, winter or summer, the sage-leaves change but little. Olive-green is
not so clear, though it has come by use to stand for a
brownish green, like the glass of a wine-bottle held up
to the light, but perhaps bottle-green is the better word.
And it is not clear what part or condition of the olive is
meant, for the ripe fruit is nearly black, and the tree in
general, and the leaf in detail, are of a cool-grey colour.
Perhaps the colour-word is taken from the colour of the
unripe fruit pickled in brine, as we see them on the table.
Grass-green any one may understand, but I am always
puzzled by apple-green. Apples are of so many different
greens, to say nothing of red and yellow; and as for
pea-green, I have no idea what it means.

I notice in plant-lists the most reckless and indiscrimi-
nate use of the words purple, violet, mauve, lilac, and
lavender, and as they are all related, I think they should
be used with the greater caution. I should say that mauve
and lilac cover the same ground; the word mauve came

into use within my recollection. It is French for mallow, and the flower of the wild plant may stand as the type of what the word means. Lavender stands for a colder or bluer range of pale purples, with an inclination to grey; it is a useful word, because the whole colour of the flower spike varies so little. Violet stands for the dark garden violet, and I always think of the grand colour of *Iris reticulata* as an example of a rich violet-purple. But purple equally stands for this, and for many shades redder.

Snow-white is very vague. There is nearly always so much blue about the colour of snow, from its crystalline surface and partial transparency, and the texture is so unlike that of any kind of flower, that the comparison is scarcely permissible. I take it that the use of 'snow-white' is, like that of 'golden-yellow,' more symbolical than descriptive, meaning any white that gives an impression of purity. Nearly all white flowers are yellowish-white, and the comparatively few that are bluish-white, such, for example, as *Omphalodes linifolia*, are of a texture so different from snow that one cannot compare them at all. I should say that most white flowers are near the colour of chalk; for although the word chalky-white has been used in rather a contemptuous way, the colour is really a very beautiful warm white, but by no means an intense white. The flower that always looks to me the whitest is that of *Iberis sempervirens*. The white is dead and hard, like a piece of glazed stoneware, quite without play or variation, and hence uninteresting.

5. The Scents of the Garden

The sweet scents of a garden are by no means the least of its many delights. Even January brings *Chimonanthus fragrans*, one of the sweetest and strongest scented of the year's blooms – little half-transparent yellowish bells on an otherwise naked-looking wall shrub. They have no stalks, but if they are floated in a shallow dish of water, they last well for several days, and give off a powerful fragrance in a room.

During some of the warm days that nearly always come towards the end of February, if one knows where to look in some sunny, sheltered corner of a hazel copse, there will be sure to be some Primroses, and the first scent of the year's first Primrose is no small pleasure. The garden Primroses soon follow, and, meanwhile, in all open winter weather there have been Czar Violets and *Iris stylosa*, with its delicate scent, faintly violet-like, but with a dash of tulip. *Iris reticulata* is also sweet, with a still stronger perfume of the violet character. But of all Irises I know, the sweetest to smell is a later blooming one, *I. graminea*. Its small purple flowers are almost hidden among the thick mass of grassy foliage which rises high above the bloom; but they are worth looking for, for the sake of the sweet and rather penetrating scent, which is exactly like that of a perfectly-ripened plum.

All the scented flowers of the Primrose tribe are delightful – Primrose, Polyanthus, Auricula, Cowslip. The actual sweetness is most apparent in the Cowslip; in the Auricula it has a pungency, and at the same time a kind of veiled mystery, that accords with the clouded and curiously-blended colourings of many of the flowers.

Sweetbriar is one of the strongest of the year's early scents, and closely following is the woodland incense of the Larch, both freely given off and far-wafted, as is also that of the hardy Daphnes. The first quarter of the year also brings the bloom of most of the deciduous Magnolias, all with a fragrance nearly allied to that of the large one that blooms late in summer, but not so strong and heavy.

The sweetness of a sun-baked bank of Wallflower belongs to April. Daffodils, lovely as they are, must be classed among flowers of rather rank smell, and yet it is welcome, for it means spring-time, with its own charm and its glad promise of the wealth of summer bloom that is soon to come. The scent of the Jonquil, Poeticus, and Polyanthus sections are best, Jonquil perhaps best of all, for it is without the rather coarse scent of the Trumpets and Nonsuch, and also escapes the penetrating lusciousness of *poeticus* and *Tazetta*, which in the south of Europe is exaggerated in the case of *tazetta* into something distinctly unpleasant.

What a delicate refinement there is in the scent of the wild Wood-Violet; it is never overdone. It seems to me to be quite the best of all the violet-scents, just because of its temperate quality. It gives exactly enough, and never that perhaps-just-a-trifle-too-much that may often be noticed about a bunch of frame-Violets, and that also in the south is intensified to a degree that is distinctly undesirable. For just as colour may be strengthened to a painful glare, and sound may be magnified to a torture, so even a sweet scent may pass its appointed bounds and become an overpoweringly evil smell. Even in England several of the Lilies, whose smell is delicious in open-air wafts, cannot be borne in a room. In the south of Europe a Tuberose cannot be brought indoors, and even at home I remember one warm wet August how a plant of Balm of Gilead (*Cedronella triphylla*) had its always powerful but usually agreeably-aromatic smell so much exaggerated that it smelt exactly like coal-gas! A brother in Jamaica writes of the large white Jasmine: 'It does not do to bring it indoors here; the scent is too strong. One day I thought there was a dead rat under the floor (a thing which did happen once), and behold, it was a glassful of fresh white Jasmine that was the offender!'

While on this less pleasant part of the subject, I cannot help thinking of the horrible smell of the Dragon Arum; and yet how fitting an accompaniment it is to the plant, for if ever there was a plant that looked wicked and repellent, it is this; and yet, like Medusa, it has its own kind of fearful beauty. In this family the smell seems to accompany the appearance, and to diminish in unpleasantness as the flower increases in amiability; for in our native wild Arum the smell, though not exactly nice, is quite innocuous, and in the beautiful white Arum or *Calla* of our greenhouses there is as little scent as a flower can well have, especially one of such large dimensions. In Fungi the bad smell is nearly always an indication of poisonous nature, so that it would seem to be given as a warning. But it has always been a matter of wonder to me why the root of the harmless and friendly Laurustinus should have been given a particularly odious smell – a smell I would rather not attempt to describe. On moist warmish days in mid-seasons I have sometimes had a whiff of the same unpleasantness from the bushes themselves; others of the same tribe have it in a much lesser degree. There is a curious smell about the yellow roots of Berberis, not exactly nasty, and a strong odour, not really offensive, but that I personally dislike, about the root of *Chrysanthemum maximum*. On the other hand, I always enjoy digging up, dividing, and replanting the *Asarums*, both the common European and the American kinds; their roots have a pleasant and most interesting smell, a good deal like mild pepper and ginger mixed, but more strongly aromatic. The same class of smell, but much fainter, and always reminding me of very good and delicate pepper, I enjoy in the flowers of the perennial Lupines. The only other hardy flowers I can think of whose smell is distinctly offensive are *Lilium pyrenaicum*, smelling like a mangy dog, and some of the *Schizanthus*, that are redolent of dirty hen-house.

There is a class of scent that, though it can neither be called sweet nor aromatic, is decidedly pleasing and interesting. Such is that of Bracken and other Fern-fronds, Ivy-leaves, Box-bushes, Vine-blossom, Elder-flowers, and Fig-leaves. There are the sweet scents that are wholly delightful – most of the Roses, Honeysuckle,

Primrose, Cowslip, Mignonette, Pink, Carnation, Heliotrope, Lily of the Valley, and a host of others; then there
is a class of scent that is intensely powerful, and gives an
impression almost of intemperance or voluptuousness,
such as Magnolia, Tuberose, Gardenia, Stephanotis, and
Jasmine; it is strange that these all have white flowers of
thick leathery texture. In strongest contrast to these are
the sweet, wholesome, wind-wafted scents of clover-
field, of bean-field, and of new-mown hay, and the soft
honey-scent of sun-baked heather, and of a buttercup
meadow in April. Still more delicious is the wind-swept
sweetness of a wood of Larch or of Scotch Fir, and the
delicate perfume of young-leaved Birch, or the heavier
scent of the flowering Lime. Out on the moorlands,
besides the sweet heather-scent, is that of flowering
Broom and Gorse and of the Bracken, so like the first
smell of the sea as you come near it after a long absence.

How curiously scents of flowers and leaves fall into
classes – often one comes upon related smells running
into one another in not necessarily related plants. There
is a kind of scent that I sometimes meet with about
clumps of Brambles, a little like the waft of a Fir wood;
it occurs again (quite naturally) in the first taste of black-
berry jam, and then turns up again in Sweet Sultan. It is
allied to the smell of the dying Strawberry leaves.

The smell of the Primrose occurs again in a much
stronger and ranker form in the root-stock, and the same
thing happens with the Violets and Pansies; in Violets
the plant-smell is pleasant, though without the high
perfume of the flower; but the smell of an overgrown
bed of Pansy-plants is rank to offensiveness.

Perhaps the most delightful of all flower scents are those whose tender and delicate quality makes one wish for just a little more. Such a scent is that of Apple-blossom, and of some small Pansies, and of the wild Rose and the Honeysuckle. Among Roses alone the variety and degree of sweet scent seems almost infinite. To me the sweetest of all is the Provence, the old Cabbage Rose of our gardens. When something approaching this appears, as it frequently does, among the hybrid perpetuals, I always greet it as the real sweet Rose smell. One expects every Rose to be fragrant, and it is a disappointment to find that such a beautiful flower as Baroness Rothschild is wanting in the sweet scent that would be the fitting complement of its incomparable form, and to perceive in so handsome a Rose as Malmaison a heavy smell of decidedly bad quality. But such cases are not frequent.

There is much variety in the scent of the Tea-Roses, the actual tea flavour being strongest in the Dijon class. Some have a powerful scent that is very near that of a ripe Nectarine; of this the best example I know is the old rose Goubault. The half-double red Gloire de Rosamène has a delightful scent of a kind that is rare among Roses. It has a good deal of the quality of that mysterious and delicious smell given off by the dying strawberry leaves, aromatic, pungent, and delicately refined, searching and powerful, and yet subtle and elusive – the best sweet smell of all the year. One cannot have it for the seeking; it comes as it will – a scent that is sad as a forecast of the inevitable certainty of the flower-year's waning, and yet sweet with the promise of its timely new birth.

Sometimes I have met with a scent of somewhat the same mysterious and aromatic kind when passing near a bank clothed with the great St John's Wort. As this also occurs in early autumn, I suppose it to be occasioned by the decay of some of the leaves. And there is a small yellow-flowered Potentilla that has a scent of the same character, but always freely and willingly given off – a humble-looking little plant, well worth growing for its sweetness, that much to my regret I have lost.

I observe that when a Rose exists in both single and double form the scent is increased in the double beyond the proportion that one would expect. *Rosa lucida* in the ordinary single state has only a very slight scent; in the lovely double form it is very sweet, and has acquired somewhat of the Moss-rose smell. The wild Burnet-rose (*R. spinosissima*) has very little smell; but the Scotch Briars, its garden relatives, have quite a powerful fragrance, a pale flesh-pink kind, whose flowers are very round and globe-like, being the sweetest of all.

But of all the sweet scents of bush or flower, the ones that give me the greatest pleasure are those of the aromatic class, where they seem to have a wholesome resinous or balsamic base, with a delicate perfume added. When I pick and crush in my hand a twig of Bay, or brush against a bush of Rosemary, or tread upon a tuft of Thyme, or pass through incense-laden brakes of Cistus, I feel that here is all that is best and purest and most refined, and nearest to poetry, in the range of faculty of the sense of smell.

The scents of all these sweet shrubs, many of them at home in dry and rocky places in far-away lower latitudes, recall in a way far more distinct than can be done by a mere mental effort of recollection, rambles of years ago in many a lovely southern land – in the islands of the Greek Archipelago, beautiful in form, and from a distance looking bare and arid, and yet with a scattered growth of lowly, sweet-smelling bush and herb, so that as you move among them every plant seems full of sweet sap or aromatic gum, and as you tread the perfumed carpet the whole air is scented; then of dusky groves of tall Cypress and Myrtle, forming mysterious shadowy woodland temples that unceasingly offer up an incense of their own surpassing fragrance, and of cooler hollows in the same lands and in the nearer Orient, where the Oleander grows like the willow of the north, and where the Sweet Bay throws up great tree-like suckers of surprising strength and vigour. It is only when one has seen it grow like this that one can appreciate the full force of the old Bible simile. Then to find oneself standing (while still on earth) in a grove of giant Myrtles fifteen feet high, is like having a little chink of the door of heaven opened, as if to show a momentary glimpse of what good things may be beyond!

Among the sweet shrubs from the nearer of these southern regions, one of the best for English gardens is *Cistus laurifolius*. Its wholesome, aromatic sweetness is freely given off, even in winter. In this, as in its near relative, *C. ladaniferus*, the scent seems to come from the gummy surface, and not from the body of the leaf. *Caryopteris Mastacanthus*, the Mastic plant, from China, one of the few shrubs that flower in autumn, has strongly-scented woolly leaves, something like turpentine, but more refined. *Ledum palustre* has a delightful scent when its leaves are bruised. The wild Bog-myrtle, so common in Scotland, has almost the sweetness of the true Myrtle, as has also the broad-leaved North American kind, and the Sweet Fern-bush (*Comptonia asplenifolia*) from the same country. The myrtle-leaved Rhododendron is a dwarf shrub of neat habit, whose bruised leaves have also a myrtle-like smell, though it is less strong than in the Gales. I wonder why the leaves of nearly all the hardy aromatic shrubs are of a hard, dry texture; the exceptions are so few that it seems to be a law.

If my copse were some acres larger I should like nothing better than to make a good-sized clearing, lying out to the sun, and to plant it with these aromatic bushes and herbs. The main planting should be of Cistus and Rosemary and Lavender, and for the shadier edges the Myrtle-leaved Rhododendron, and *Ledum palustre*, and the three Bog-myrtles. Then again in the sun would be Hyssop and Catmint, and Lavender-cotton and Southernwood, with others of the scented Artemisias, and Sage and Marjoram. All the ground would be carpeted with Thyme and Basil and others of the dwarfer sweet-herbs. There would be no regular paths, but it would be so planted that in most parts one would have to brush up against the sweet bushes, and sometimes push through them, as one does on the thinner-clothed of the mountain slopes of southern Italy.

Among the many wonders of the vegetable world are the flowers that hang their heads and seem to sleep in the daytime, and that awaken as the sun goes down, and live their waking life at night. And those that are most familiar in our gardens have powerful perfumes, except the Evening Primrose (*Œnothera*), which has only a milder sweetness. It is vain to try and smell the night-given scent in the daytime; it is either withheld altogether, or some other smell, quite different, and not always pleasant, is there instead. I have tried hard in daytime to get a whiff of the night sweetness of *Nicotiana affinis*, but can only get hold of something that smells like a horse! Some of the best of the night-scents are those given by the Stocks and Rockets. They are sweet in the hand in the daytime, but the best of the sweet scent seems to be like a thin film on the surface. It does not do to smell them too vigorously, for, especially in Stocks and Wallflowers, there is a strong, rank, cabbage-like under-smell. But in the sweetness given off so freely in the summer evening there is none of this; then they only give their very best.

But of all the family, the finest fragrance comes from the small annual Night-scented Stock (*Matthiola bicornis*), a plant that in daytime is almost ugly; for the leaves are of a dull-grey colour, and the flowers are small and also dull-coloured, and they are closed and droop and look unhappy. But when the sun has set the modest little plant seems to come to life; the grey foliage is almost beautiful in its harmonious relation to the half-light; the flowers stand up and expand, and in the early twilight show tender colouring of faint pink and lilac, and pour out upon the still night-air a lavish gift of sweetest fragrance; and the modest little plant that in strong sunlight looked unworthy of a place in the garden, now rises to its appointed rank and reigns supreme as its prime delight.

6. The Worship of False Gods

Several times during these notes I have spoken in a disparaging manner of the show-table; and I have not done so lightly, but with all the care and thought and power of observation that my limited capacity is worth; and, broadly, I have come to this: that shows, such as those at the fortnightly meetings of the Royal Horticultural Society, and their more important one in the early summer, whose object is to bring together beautiful flowers of all kinds, to a place where they may be seen, are of the utmost value; and that any shows anywhere for a like purpose, and especially where there are no money prizes, are also sure to be helpful. And the test question I put to myself at any show is this, Does this really help the best interests of horticulture? And as far as I can see that it does this, I think the show right and helpful; and whenever it does not, I think it harmful and misleading.

The love of gardening has so greatly grown and spread within the last few years, that the need of really good and beautiful garden flowers is already far in advance of the demand for the so-called 'florists' flowers, by which I mean those that find favour in the exclusive shows of Societies for the growing and exhibition of such flowers as Tulips, Carnations, Dahlias, and Chrysanthemums. In support of this I should like to know what proportion of demand there is, in Dahlias, for instance, between the show kinds, whose aim and object is the show-table, and the decorative kinds, that are indisputably better for garden use. Looking at the catalogue of a leading Dahlia nursery, I find that the decorative kinds fill ten pages, while the show kinds, including Pompones, fill only three. Is not this some indication of what is wanted in gardens?

I am of opinion that the show-table is unworthily used when its object is to be an end in itself, and that it should be only a means to a better end, and that when it exhibits what has become merely a 'fancy,' it loses sight of its honourable position as a trustworthy exponent of horti-culture, and has degenerated to a baser use. When, as in Chrysanthemum shows, the flowers on the board are of *no use anywhere but on that board*, and for the purpose of gaining a money prize, I hold that the show-table has a debased aim, and a debasing influence. Beauty, in all the best sense, is put aside in favour of set rules and measurements, and the production of a thing that is of no use or value; and individuals of a race of plants capable of producing the highest and most delightful forms of beauty, and of brightening our homes, and even gardens, during the dim days of early winter, are teased and tortured and fatted and bloated into ugly and useless monstrosities for no purpose but to gain money. And when private gardeners go to these shows and see how the prizes are awarded, and how all the glory is accorded to the first-prize bloated monster, can we wonder that the effect on their minds is confusing, if not absolutely harmful?

Shows of Carnations and Pansies, where the older rules prevail, are equally misleading, where the single flowers are arranged in a flat circle of paper. As with the Chrysanthemum, every sort of trickery is allowed in arranging the petals of the Carnation blooms: petals are pulled out or stuck in, and they are twisted about, and groomed and combed, and manipulated with special tools – 'dressed,' as the show-word has it – dressed so elaborately that the dressing only stops short of applying actual paint and perfumery. Already in the case of Carnations a better influence is being felt, and at the London shows there are now classes for border Carnations set up in long-stalked bunches just as they grow. It is only like this that their value as outdoor plants can be tested; for many of the show sorts have miserably weak stalks, and a very poor, lanky habit of growth.

Then the poor Pansies have single blooms laid flat on white papers, and are only approved if they will lie quite flat and show an outline of a perfect circle. All that is most beautiful in a Pansy, the wing-like curves, the waved or slightly fluted radiations, the scarcely perceptible undulation of surface that displays to perfection the admirable delicacy of velvety texture; all the little tender tricks and ways that make the Pansy one of the best-loved of garden flowers; all this is overlooked, and not only passively overlooked, but overtly contemned. The show-pansy judge appears to have no eye, or brain, or heart, but to have in their place a pair of compasses with which to describe a circle! All idea of garden delight seems to be excluded, as this kind of judging appeals to no recognition of beauty for beauty's sake, but to hard systems of measurement and rigid arrangement and computation that one would think more applicable to astronomy or geometry than to any matter relating to horticulture.

I do most strongly urge that beauty of the highest class should be the aim, and not anything of the nature of fashion or 'fancy,' and that every effort should be made towards the raising rather than the lowering of the standard of taste.

The Societies which exist throughout the country are well organised; many have existed for a great number of years; they are the local sources of horticultural education, to which large circles of people naturally look for guidance; and though they produce – especially at the Rose shows – quantities of beautiful things, it cannot but be perceived by all who have had the benefit of some refinement of education, that in very many cases they either deliberately teach, or at any rate allow to be seen with their sanction, what cannot fail to be debasing to public taste.

I will take just two examples to show how obvious methods of leading taste are not only overlooked, but even perverted; for it is not only in the individual blooms that much of the show-teaching is unworthy, but also in the training of the plants; so that a plant that by nature has some beauty of form, is not encouraged or even allowed to develop that beauty, but is trained into some shape that is not only foreign to its own nature, but is absolutely ugly and ungraceful, and entirely stupid. The natural habit of the Chrysanthemum is to grow in the form of several upright stems. They spring up sheaf-wise, straight upright for a time, and only bending a little outward above, to give room for the branching heads of bloom. The stems are rather stiff, because they are half woody at the base. In the case of pot-plants it would seem right only so far to stake or train them as to give the necessary support by a few sticks set a little outward at the top, so that each stem may lean a little over, after the manner of a Bamboo, when their clustered heads of flower would be given enough room, and be seen to the greatest advantage.

But at shows, the triumph of the training art seems to be to drag the poor thing round and round over an internal scaffolding of sticks, with an infinite number of ties and cross-braces, so that it makes a sort of shapeless ball, and to arrange the flowers so that they are equally spotted all over it, by tying back some almost to snapping-point, and by dragging forward others to the verge of dislocation. I have never seen anything so ugly in the way of potted plants as a certain kind of Chrysanthemum that has incurved flowers of a heavy sort of dull leaden-looking red-purple colour trained in this manner. Such a sight gives me a feeling of shame, not unmixed with wrathful indignation. I ask myself, What is it for? and I get no answer. I ask a practical gardener what it is for, and he says, 'Oh, it is one of the ways they are trained for shows.' I ask him, Does he think it pretty, or is it any use? and he says, 'Well, they think it makes a nice variety;' and when I press him further, and say I consider it a very nasty variety, and does he think nasty varieties are better than none, the question is beyond him, and he smiles vaguely and edges away, evidently thinking my conversation perplexing, and my company undesirable. I look again at the unhappy plant, and see its poor leaves fat with an unwholesome obesity, and seeming to say, We were really a good bit mildewed, but have been doctored up for the show by being crammed and stuffed with artificial aliment!

My second example is that of *Azalea indica*. What is prettier in a room than one of these in its little tree form, a true tree, with tiny trunk and wide-spreading branches, and its absurdly large and lovely flowers? Surely it is the most perfect room ornament that we can have in tree shape in a moderate-sized pot; and where else can one see a tree loaded with lovely bloom whose individual flowers have a diameter equal to five times that of the trunk?

But the show decrees that all this is wrong, and that the tiny, brittle branches must be trained stiffly round till the shape of the plant shows as a sort of cylinder. Again I ask myself, What is this for? What does it teach? Can it be really to teach with deliberate intention that instead of displaying its natural and graceful tree form it should aim at a more desirable kind of beauty, such as that of the chimney-pot or drain-pipe, and that this is so important that it is right and laudable to devote to it much time and delicate workmanship?

I cannot but think, as well as hope, that the strong influences for good that are now being brought to bear on all departments of gardening may reach this class of show, for there are already more hopeful signs in the admission of classes for groups arranged for decoration.

The prize-show system no doubt creates its own evils, because the judges, and those who frame the schedules, have been in most cases men who have a knowledge of flowers, but who are not people of culti-vated taste, and in deciding what points are to constitute the merits of a flower they have to take such qualities as are within the clearest understanding of people of average intelligence and average education – such, for instance, as size that can be measured, symmetry that can be easily estimated, thickness of petal that can be felt, and such qualities of colour as appeal most strongly to the uneducated eye; so that a flower may possess features or qualities that endow it with the highest beauty, but that exclude it, because the hard and narrow limits of the show-laws provide no means of dealing with it. It is, therefore, thrown out, not because they have any fault to find with it, but because it does not concern them; and the ordinary gardener, to whose practice it might be of the highest value, accepting the verdict of the show-judge as an infallible guide, also treats it with contempt and neglect.

Now, all this would not so much matter if it did not delude those whose taste is not sufficiently educated to enable them to form an opinion of their own in accord-ance with the best and truest standards of beauty; for I venture to repeat that what we have to look for for the benefit of our gardens, and for our own bettering and increase of happiness in those gardens, are things that are beautiful, rather than things that are round, or straight, or thick, still less than for those that are new, or curious, or astonishing. For all these false gods are among us, and many are they who are willing to worship.

7. *Novelty and Variety*

When I look back over thirty years of gardening, I see what extraordinary progress there has been, not only in the introduction of good plants new to general culti-vation, but also in the home production of improved kinds of old favourites. In annual plants alone there has been a remarkable advance. And here again, though many really beautiful things are being brought forward, there seems always to be an undue value assigned to a fresh development, on the score of its novelty.

Now it seems to me, that among the thousands of beautiful things already at hand for garden use, there is no merit whatever in novelty or variety unless the thing new or different is distinctly more beautiful, or in some such way better than an older thing of the same class.

And there seems to be a general wish among seed growers just now to dwarf all annual plants. Now, when a plant is naturally of a diffuse habit, the fixing of a dwarfer variety may be a distinct gain to horticulture – it may just make a good garden plant out of one that was formerly of indifferent quality; but there seems to me to be a kind of stupidity in inferring from this that all annuals are the better for dwarfing. I take it that the bedding system has had a good deal to do with it. It no doubt enables ignorant gardeners to use a larger variety of plants as senseless colour-masses, but it is obvious that many, if not most, of the plants are individually made much uglier by the process. Take, for example, one of the dwarfest Ageratums: what a silly little dumpy, formless, pincushion of a thing it is! And then the dwarfest of the China Asters. Here is a plant (whose chief weakness already lies in a certain over-stiffness) made stiffer and more shapeless still by dwarfing and by cramming with too many petals. The Comet Asters of later years are a much-improved type of flower, with a looser shape and a certain degree of approach to grace and beauty. When this kind came out it was a noteworthy novelty, not because it was a novelty, but because it was a better and more beautiful thing. Also among the same Asters the introduction of a better class of red colouring, first of the blood-red and then of the so-called scarlet shades, was a good variety, because it was the distinct bettering of the colour of a popular race of garden-flowers, whose red and pink colourings had hitherto been of a bad and rank quality.

It is quite true that here and there the dwarf kind is a distinctly useful thing, as in the dwarf Nasturtiums. In this grand plant one is glad to have dwarf ones as well as the old trailing kinds. I even confess to a certain liking for the podgy little dwarf Snapdragons; they are ungraceful little dumpy things, but they happen to have come in some tender colourings of pale yellow and pale pink, that give them a kind of absurd prettiness, and a certain garden-value. I also look at them as a little floral joke that is harmless and not displeasing, but they cannot for a moment compare in beauty with the free-growing Snapdragon of the older type. This I always think one of the best and most interesting and admirable of garden-plants. Its beauty is lost if it is crowded up among other things in a border; it should be grown in a dry wall or steep rocky bank, where its handsome bushy growth and finely-poised spikes of bloom can be well seen.

One of the annuals that I think is entirely spoilt by dwarfing is Love-in-a-Mist, a plant I hold in high admiration. Many years ago I came upon some of it in a small garden, of a type that I thought extremely desirable, with a double flower of just the right degree of fulness, and of an unusually fine colour. I was fortunate enough to get some seed, and have never grown any other, nor have I ever seen elsewhere any that I think can compare with it.

The Zinnia is another fine annual that has been much spoilt by its would-be improvers. When a Zinnia has a hard, stiff, tall flower, with a great many rows of petals piled up one on top of another, and when its habit is dwarfed to a mean degree of squatness, it looks to me both ugly and absurd, whereas a reasonably double one, well branched, and two feet high, is a handsome plant.

I also think that Stocks and Wallflowers are much handsomer when rather tall and branching. Dwarf Stocks, moreover, are invariably spattered with soil in heavy autumn rain.

An example of the improver not knowing where to stop in the matter of colouring, always strikes me in the Gaillardias, and more especially in the perennial kind, that is increased by division as well as by seed. The flower is naturally of a strong orange-yellow colour, with a narrow ring of red round the centre. The improver has sought to increase the width of the red ring. Up to a certain point it makes a livelier and brighter-looking flower; but he has gone too far, and extended the red till it has become a red flower with a narrow yellow edge. The red also is of a rather dull and heavy nature, so that instead of a handsome yellow flower with a broad central ring, here is an ugly red one with a yellow border. There is no positive harm done, as the plant has been propagated at every stage of development, and one may choose what one will; but to see them together is an instructive lesson.

No annual plant has of late years been so much improved as the Sweet Pea, and one reason why its charming beauty and scent are so enjoyable is, that they grow tall, and can be seen on a level with the eye. There can be no excuse whatever for dwarfing this, as has lately been done. There are already plenty of good flowering plants under a foot high, and the little dwarf white monstrosity, now being followed by coloured ones of the same habit, seems to me worthy of nothing but condemnation. It would be as right and sensible to dwarf a Hollyhock into a podgy mass a foot high, or a Pentstemon, or a Foxglove. Happily these have as yet escaped dwarfing, though I regret to see that a deformity that not unfrequently appears among garden Foxgloves, looking like a bell-shaped flower topping a stunted spike, appears to have been 'fixed,' and is being offered as a 'novelty.' Here is one of the clearest examples of a new development which is a distinct debasement of a naturally beautiful form, but which is nevertheless being pushed forward in trade: it has no merit whatever in itself, and is only likely to sell because it is new and curious.

And all this parade of distortion and deformity comes about from the grower losing sight of beauty as the first consideration, or from his not having the knowledge that would enable him to determine what are the points of character in various plants most deserving of development, and in not knowing when or where to stop. Abnormal size, whether greatly above or much below the average, appeals to the vulgar and uneducated eye, and will always command its attention and wonderment. But then the production of the immense size that provokes astonishment, and the misapplied ingenuity that produces unusual dwarfing, are neither of them very high aims.

And much as I feel grateful to those who improve garden flowers, I venture to repeat my strong conviction that their efforts in selection and other methods should be so directed as to keep in view the attainment of beauty in the first place, and as a point of honour; not to mere increase of size of bloom or compactness of habit – many plants have been spoilt by excess of both; not for variety or novelty as ends in themselves, but only to welcome them, and offer them, if they are distinctly of garden value in the best sense. For if plants are grown or advertised or otherwise pushed on any other account than that of their possessing some worthy form of beauty, they become of the same nature as any other article in trade that is got up for sale for the sole benefit of the seller, that is unduly lauded by advertisement, and that makes its first appeal to the vulgar eye by an exaggerated and showy pictorial representation; that will serve no useful purpose, and for which there is no true or healthy demand.

No doubt much of it comes about from the unwholesome pressure of trade competition, which in a way obliges all to follow where some lead. I trust that my many good friends in the trade will understand that my remarks are not made in any personal sense whatever. I know that some of them feel much as I do on some of these points, but that in many ways they are helpless, being all bound in a kind of bondage to the general system. And there is one great evil that calls loudly for redress, but that will endure until some of the mightiest of them have the energy and courage to band themselves together and to declare that it shall no longer exist among them.

8. Weeds and Pests

Weeding is a delightful occupation, especially after summer rain, when the roots come up clear and clean. One gets to know how many and various are the ways of weeds – as many almost as the moods of human creatures. How easy and pleasant to pull up are the soft annuals like Chickweed and Groundsel, and how one looks with respect at deep-rooted things like Docks, that make one go and fetch a spade. Comfrey is another thing with a terrible root, and every bit must be got out, as it will grow again from the smallest scrap. And hard to get up are the two Bryonies, the green and the black, with such deep-reaching roots, that, if not weeded up within their first year, will have to be seriously dug out later. The white Convolvulus, one of the loveliest of native plants, has a most persistently running root, of which every joint will quickly form a new plant. Some of the worst weeds to get out are Goutweed and Coltsfoot. Though I live on a light soil, comparatively easy to clean, I have done some gardening in clay, and well know what a despairing job it is to get the bits of either of these roots out of the stiff clods.

The most persistent weed in my soil is the small running Sheep's Sorrel. First it makes a patch, and then sends out thready running roots all round, a foot or more long; these, if not checked, establish new bases of operation, and so it goes on, always spreading farther and farther. When this happens in soft ground that can be hoed and weeded it matters less, but in the lawn it is a more serious matter. Its presence always denotes a poor, sandy soil of rather a sour quality.

Goutweed is a pest in nearly all gardens, and very difficult to get out. When it runs into the root of some patch of hardy plant, if the plant can be spared, I find it best to send it at once to the burn-heap; or if it is too precious, there is nothing for it but to cut it all up and wash it out, to be sure that not the smallest particle of the enemy remains. Some weeds are deceiving – Sow-thistle, for instance, which has the look of promising firm hand-hold and easy extraction, but has a disappointing way of almost always breaking short off at the collar. But of all the garden weeds that are native plants I know none so persistent or so insidious as the Rampion Bell-flower (*Campanula rapunculoides*); it grows from the smallest thread of root, and it is almost impossible to see every little bit; for though the main roots are thick, and white, and fleshy, the fine side roots that run far abroad are very small, and of a reddish colour, and easily hidden in the brown earth.

But some of the worst garden-weeds are exotics run wild. The common Grape Hyacinth sometimes overruns a garden and cannot be got rid of. *Sambucus Ebulus* is a plant to beware of, its long thong-like roots spreading far and wide, and coming up again far away from the parent stock. For this reason it is valuable for planting in such places as newly-made pond-heads, helping to tie the bank together. *Polygonum Sieboldi* must also be planted with caution. The winter Heliotrope (*Petasites fragrans*) is almost impossible to get out when once it has taken hold, growing in the same way as its near relative the native Coltsfoot.

But by far the most difficult plant to abolish or even keep in check that I know is *Ornithogalum nutans*. Beautiful as it is, and valuable as a cut flower, I will not have it in the garden. I think I may venture to say that in this soil, when once established, it cannot be eradicated. Each mature bulb makes a host of offsets, and the seed quickly ripens. When it is once in a garden it will suddenly appear in all sorts of different places. It is no use trying to dig it out. I have dug out the whole space of soil containing the patch, a barrow-load at a time, and sent it to the middle of the burn-heap, and put in fresh soil, and there it is again next year, nearly as thick as ever. I have dug up individual small patches with the greatest care, and got out every bulb and offset, and every bit of the whitish leaf stem, for I have such faith in its power of reproduction that I think every atom of this is capable of making a plant, only to find next year a thriving young tuft of the 'grass' in the same place. And yet the bulb and underground stem are white, and the earth is brown, and I passed it all several times through my fingers, but all in vain. I confess that it beats me entirely.

Coronilla varia is a little plant that appears in catalogues among desirable Alpines, but is a very 'rooty' and troublesome thing, and scarcely good enough for garden use, though pretty in a grassy bank where its rambling ways would not be objectionable. I once brought home from Brittany some roots of *Linaria repens*, that looked charming by a roadside, and planted them in a bit of Alpine garden, a planting that I never afterwards ceased to regret.

I learnt from an old farmer a good way of getting rid of a bed of nettles – to thrash them down with a stick every time they grow up. If this is done about three times during the year, the root becomes so much weakened that it is easily forked out, or if the treatment is gone on with, the second year the nettles die. Thrashing with a stick is better than cutting, as it makes the plant bleed more; any mutilation of bruise or ragged tearing of fibre is more harmful to plant or tree than clean cutting.

Of bird, beast, and insect pests we have plenty. First, and worst, are rabbits. They will gnaw and nibble anything and everything that is newly planted, even native things like Juniper, Scotch Fir, and Gorse. The necessity of wiring everything newly planted adds greatly to the labour and expense of the garden, and the unsightly grey wire-netting is an unpleasant eyesore. When plants or bushes are well established the rabbits leave them alone, though some families of plants are always irresistible – Pinks and Carnations, for instance, and nearly all *Cruciferæ*, such as Wallflowers, Stocks, and Iberis. The only plants I know that they do not touch are Rhododendrons and Azaleas; they leave them for the hare, that is sure to get in every now and then, and who stands up on his long hindlegs, and will eat Rose-bushes quite high up.

Plants eaten by a hare look as if they had been cut

with a sharp knife; there is no appearance of gnawing or nibbling, no ragged edges of wood or frayed bark, but just a straight clean cut.

Field mice are very troublesome. Some years they will nibble off the flower-buds of the Lent Hellebores; when they do this they have a curious way of collecting them and laying them in heaps. I have no idea why they do this, as they neither carry them away nor eat them afterwards; there the heaps of buds lie till they rot or dry up. They once stole all my Auricula seed in the same way. I had marked some good plants for seed, cutting off all the other flowers as soon as they went out of bloom. The seed was ripening, and I watched it daily, awaiting the moment for harvesting. But a few days before it was ready I went round and found the seed was all gone; it had been cut off at the top of the stalk, so that the umbel-shaped heads had been taken away whole. I looked about, and luckily found three slightly hollow places under the bank at the back of the border where the seed-heads had been piled in heaps. In this case it looked as if it had been stored for food; luckily it was near enough to ripeness for me to save my crop.

The mice are also troublesome with newly sown Peas, eating some underground, while sparrows nibble off others when just sprouted; and when outdoor Grapes are ripening mice run up the walls and eat them. Even when the Grapes are tied in oiled canvas bags they will eat through the bags to get at them, though I have never known them to gnaw through the newspaper bags that I now use in preference, and that ripen the Grapes as well. I am not sure whether it is mice or birds that pick off the flowers of the big bunch Primroses, but am inclined to think it is mice, because the stalks are cut low down.

Pheasants are very bad gardeners; what they seem to enjoy most are Crocuses – in fact, it is no use planting them. I had once a nice collection of Crocus species. They were in separate patches, all along the edge of one border, in a sheltered part of the garden, where pheasants did not often come. One day when I came to see my Crocuses, I found where each patch had been a basin-shaped excavation and a few fragments of stalk or some part of the plant. They had begun at one end and worked steadily along, clearing them right out. They also destroyed a long bed of *Anemone fulgens*. First they took the flowers, and then the leaves, and lastly pecked up and ate the roots.

But we have one grand consolation in having no slugs, at least hardly any that are truly indigenous; they do not like our dry, sandy heaths. Friends are very generous in sending them with plants, so that we have a moderate number that hang about frames and pot plants, though nothing much to boast of; but they never trouble seed-lings in the open ground, and for this I can never be too thankful.

Alas that the beautiful bullfinch should be so dire an enemy to fruit-trees, and also the pretty little tits! but so it is; and it is a sad sight to see a well-grown fruit-tree with all its fruit-buds pecked out and lying under it on the ground in a thin green carpet. We had some fine young cherry-trees in a small orchard that we cut down in despair after they had been growing twelve years. They were too large to net, and their space could not be spared just for the mischievous fun of the birds.

9. The Bedding Fashion and Its Influence

It is curious to look back at the old days of bedding-out, when that and that only meant gardening to most people, and to remember how the fashion, beginning in the larger gardens, made its way like a great inundating wave, submerging the lesser ones, and almost drowning out the beauties of the many little flowery cottage plots of our English waysides. And one wonders how it all came about, and why the bedding system, admirable for its own purpose, should have thus out-stepped its bounds, and have been allowed to run riot among gardens great and small throughout the land. But so it was, and for many years the fashion, for it was scarcely anything better, reigned supreme.

It was well for all real lovers of flowers when some quarter of a century ago a strong champion of the good old flowers arose, and fought strenuously to stay the devastating tide, and to restore the healthy liking for the good old garden flowers. Many soon followed, and now one may say that all England has flocked to the standard. Bedding as an all-prevailing fashion is now dead; the old garden-flowers are again honoured and loved, and every encouragement is freely offered to those who will improve old kinds and bring forward others.

And now that bedding as a fashion no longer exists, one can look at it more quietly and fairly, and see what its uses really are, for in its own place and way it is undoubtedly useful and desirable. Many great country-houses are only inhabited in winter, then perhaps for a week or two at Easter, and in the late summer. There is probably a house-party at Easter, and a succession of visitors in the late summer. A brilliant garden, visible from the house, dressed for spring and dressed for early autumn, is exactly what is wanted – not necessarily from any special love of flowers, but as a kind of bright and well-kept furnishing of the immediate environment of the house. The gardener delights in it; it is all routine work; so many hundreds or thousands of scarlet Geranium, of yellow Calceolaria, of blue Lobelia, of golden Feverfew, or of other coloured material. It wants no imagination; the comprehension of it is within the range of the most limited understanding; indeed its prevalence for some twenty years or more must have had a deteriorating influence on the whole class of private gardeners, presenting to them an ideal so easy of attainment and so cheap of mental effort.

But bedding, though it is gardening of the least poetical or imaginative kind, can be done badly or beautifully. In the *parterre* of the formal garden it is absolutely in place, and brilliantly-beautiful pictures can be made by a wise choice of colouring. I once saw, and can never forget, a bedded garden that was a perfectly satisfying example of colour-harmony; but then it was planned by the master, a man of the most refined taste, and not by the gardener. It was a *parterre* that formed part of the garden in one of the fine old places in the Midland counties. I have no distinct recollection of the design, except that there was some principle of fan-shaped radiation, of which each extreme angle formed one centre. The whole garden was treated in one harmonious colouring of full yellow, orange, and orange-brown; half-hardy annuals, such as French and African Marigolds, Zinnias, and Nasturtiums, being freely used. It was the most noble treatment of one limited range of colouring I have ever seen in a garden; brilliant without being garish, and sumptuously gorgeous without the reproach of gaudiness – a precious lesson in temperance and restraint in the use of the one colour, and an admirable exposition of its powerful effect in the hands of a true artist.

I think that in many smaller gardens a certain amount of bedding may be actually desirable; for where the owner of a garden has a special liking for certain classes or mixtures of plants, or wishes to grow them thoroughly well and enjoy them individually to the full, he will naturally grow them in separate beds, or may intentionally combine the beds, if he will, into some form of good garden effect. But the great fault of the bedding system when at its height was, that it swept over the country as a tyrannical fashion, that demanded, and for the time being succeeded in effecting, the exclusion of better and more thoughtful kinds of gardening; for I believe I am right in saying that it spread like an epidemic disease, and raged far and wide for nearly a quarter of a century.

Its worst form of all was the 'ribbon border,' generally a line of scarlet Geranium at the back, then a line of

Calceolaria, then a line of blue Lobelia, and lastly, a line of the inevitable Golden Feather Feverfew, or what our gardener used to call Featherfew. Could anything be more tedious or more stupid? And the ribbon border was at its worst when its lines were not straight, but waved about in weak and silly sinuations.

And when bedding as a fashion was dead, when this false god had been toppled off his pedestal, and his worshippers had been converted to better beliefs, in turning and rending him they often went too far, and did injustice to the innocent by professing a dislike to many a good plant, and renouncing its use. It was not the fault of the Geranium or of the Calceolaria that they had been grievously misused and made to usurp too large a share of our garden spaces. Not once but many a time my visitors have expressed unbounded surprise when they saw these plants in my garden, saying, 'I should have thought that you would have despised Geraniums.' On the contrary, I love Geraniums. There are no plants to come near them for pot, or box, or stone basket, or for massing in any sheltered place in hottest sunshine; and I love their strangely-pleasant smell, and their beautiful modern colourings of soft scarlet and salmon-scarlet and salmon-pink, some of these grouping beautifully together. I have a space in connection with some formal stonework of steps, and tank, and paved walks, close to the house, on purpose for the summer placing of large pots of Geranium, with sometimes a few Cannas and Lilies. For a quarter of the year it is one of the best things in the garden, and delightful in colour. Then no plant does so well or looks so suitable in some earthen pots and boxes from Southern Italy that I always think the best that were ever made, their shape and well-designed ornament traditional from the Middle Ages, and probably from an even more remote antiquity.

There are, of course, among bedding Geraniums many of a bad, raw quality of colour, particularly among cold, hard pinks, but there are so many to choose from that these can easily be avoided.

I remember some years ago, when the bedding fashion was going out, reading some rather heated discussions in the gardening papers about methods of planting out and arranging various tender but indispensable plants. Some one who had been writing about the errors of the bedding system wrote about planting some of these in isolated masses. He was pounced upon by another, who asked, 'What is this but bedding?' The second writer was so far justified, in that it cannot be denied that any planting in beds is bedding. But then there is bedding and bedding – a right and a wrong way of applying the treatment. Another matter that roused the combative spirit of the captious critic was the filling up of bare spaces in mixed borders with Geraniums, Calceolarias, and other such plants. Again he said, 'What is this but bedding? These are bedding plants.' When I read this it seemed to me that his argument was, These plants may be very good plants in themselves, but because they have for some years been used wrongly, therefore they must not now be used rightly! In the case of my own visitors, when they have expressed surprise at my having 'those horrid old bedding plants' in my garden, it seemed quite a new view when I pointed out that bedding plants were only passive agents in their own misuse, and that a Geranium was a Geranium long before it was a bedding plant! But the discussion raised in my mind a wish to come to some conclusion about the difference between bedding in the better and worse sense, in relation to the cases quoted, and it appeared to me to be merely in the choice between right and wrong placing – placing monotonously or stupidly, so as merely to fill the space, or placing with a feeling for 'drawing' or proportion. For I had very soon found out that, if I had a number of things to plant anywhere, whether only to fill up a border or as a detached group, if I placed the things myself, carefully exercising what power of discrimination I might have acquired, it looked fairly right, but that if I left it to one of my garden people (a thing I rarely do) it looked all nohow, or like bedding in the worst sense of the word.

Even the better ways of gardening do not wholly escape the debasing influence of fashion. Wild gardening is a delightful, and in good hands a most desirable, pursuit, but no kind of gardening is so difficult to do well, or is so full of pitfalls and of paths of peril. Because it has in some measure become fashionable, and because it is understood to mean the planting of exotics in wild places, unthinking people rush to the conclusion that they can put any garden plants into any wild places, and that that is wild gardening. I have seen woody places that were already perfect with their own simple charm just muddled and spoilt by a reckless planting of garden refuse, and heathy hillsides already sufficiently and beautifully clothed with native vegetation made to look lamentably silly by the planting of a nurseryman's mixed lot of exotic Conifers.

In my own case, I have always devoted the most careful consideration to any bit of wild gardening I thought of doing, never allowing myself to decide upon it till I felt thoroughly assured that the place seemed to ask for the planting in contemplation, and that it would be distinctly a gain in pictorial value; so there are stretches of Daffodils in one part of the copse, while another is carpeted with Lily of the Valley. A cool bank is covered with Gaultheria, and just where I thought they would look well as little jewels of beauty, are spreading patches of Trillium and the great yellow Dog-tooth Violet. Besides these there are only some groups of the Giant Lily. Many other exotic plants could have been made to grow in the wooded ground, but they did not seem to be wanted; I thought where the copse looked well and complete in itself it was better left alone.

But where the wood joins the garden some bold groups of flowering plants are allowed, as of Mullein in one part and Foxglove in another; for when standing in the free part of the garden, it is pleasant to project the sight far into the wood, and to let the garden influences penetrate here and there, the better to join the one to the other.

10. Masters and Men

Now that the owners of good places are for the most part taking a newly-awakened and newly-educated pleasure in the better ways of gardening, a frequent source of difficulty arises from the ignorance and obstructiveness of gardeners. The owners have become aware that their gardens may be sources of the keenest pleasure. The gardener may be an excellent man, perfectly understanding the ordinary routine of garden work; he may have been many years in his place; it is his settled home, and he is getting well on into middle life; but he has no understanding of the new order of things, and when the master, perfectly understanding what he is about, desires that certain things shall be done, and wishes to enjoy the pleasure of directing the work himself, and seeing it grow under his hand, he resents it as an interference, and becomes obstructive, or does what is required in a spirit of such sullen acquiescence that it is equal to open opposition. And I have seen so many gardens and gardeners that I have come to recognise certain types; and this one, among men of a certain age, is unfortunately frequent. Various degrees of ignorance and narrow-mindedness must no doubt be expected among the class that produces private gardeners. Their general education is not very wide to begin with, and their training is usually all in one groove, and the many who possess a full share of vanity get to think that, because they have exhausted the obvious sources of experience that have occurred within their reach, there is nothing more to learn, or to know, or to see, or to feel, or to enjoy. It is in this that the difficulty lies. The man has no doubt done his best through life; he has performed his duties well and faithfully, and can render a good account of his stewardship. It is no fault of his that more means of enlarging his mind have not been within his grasp, and, to a certain degree, he may be excused for not understanding that there is anything beyond; but if he is naturally vain and stubborn his case is hopeless. If, on the other hand, he is wise enough to know that he does not know everything, and modest enough to acknowledge it, as do all the greatest and most learned of men, he will then be eager to receive new and enlarged impressions, and his willing and intelligent co-operation will be a new source of interest in life both to himself and his employer, as well as a fresh spring of vitality in the life of the garden. I am speaking of the large middle class of private gardeners, not of those of the highest rank, who have among them men of good education and a large measure of refinement. From among these I think of the late Mr Ingram of the Belvoir Castle gardens, with regret as for a personal friend, and also as of one who was a true garden artist.

But most people who have fair-sized gardens have to do with the middle class of gardener, the man of narrow mental training. The master who, after a good many

years of active life, is looking forward to settling in his
home and improving and enjoying his garden, has had
so different a training, a course of teaching so immeasur-
ably wider and more enlightening. As a boy he was in a
great public school, where, by wholesome friction with
his fellows, he had any petty or personal nonsense
knocked out of him while still in his early 'teens.' Then
he goes to college, and whether studiously inclined or
not, he is already in the great world, always widening
his ideas and experience. Then perhaps he is in one
of the active professions, or engaged in scientific or
intellectual research, or in diplomacy, his ever-expanding
intelligence rubbing up against all that is most enlightened and astute in men, or most profoundly inexplicable
in matter. He may be at the same time cultivating his
taste for literature and the fine arts, searching the libraries
and galleries of the civilised world for the noblest and
most divinely inspired examples of human work; seeing
with an eye that daily grows more keenly searching, and
receiving and holding with a brain that ever gains a
firmer grasp, and so acquires some measure of the higher
critical faculty. He sees the ruined gardens of antiquity,
colossal works of the rulers of Imperial Rome, and the
later gardens of the Middle Ages (direct descendants of
those greater and older ones), some of them still among
the most beautiful gardens on earth. He sees how the
taste for gardening grew and travelled, spreading
through Europe and reaching England, first, no doubt,
through her Roman invaders. He becomes more and
more aware of what great and enduring happiness may
be enjoyed in a garden, and how all that he can learn of

it in the leisure intervals of his earlier maturity, and then in middle life, will help to brighten his later days, when he hopes to refine and make better the garden of the old home by a reverent application of what he has learnt. He thinks of the desecrated old bowling-green, cut up to suit the fashion of thirty years ago into a patchwork of incoherent star and crescent shaped beds; of how he will give it back its ancient character of unbroken repose; he thinks how he will restore the string of fish-ponds in the bottom of the wooded valley just below, now a rushy meadow with swampy hollows that once were ponds, and humpy mounds, ruins of the ancient dikes; of how the trees will stand reflected in the still water; and how he will live to see again in middle hours of summer days, as did the monks of old, the broad backs of the golden carp basking just below the surface of the sun-warmed water.

And such a man as this comes home some day and finds the narrow-minded gardener, who believes that he already knows all that can be known about gardening, who thinks that the merely technical part, which he perfectly understands, is all that there is to be known and practised, and that his crude ideas about arrangement of flowers are as good as those of any one else. And a man of this temperament cannot be induced to believe, and still less can he be made to understand, that all that he knows is only the means to a further and higher end, and that what he can show of a completed garden can only reach to an average dead-level of dulness compared with what may come of the life-giving influence of one who has the mastery of the higher garden knowledge.

Moreover, he either forgets, or does not know, what is the main purpose of a garden, namely, that it is to give its owner the best and highest kind of earthly pleasure. Neither is he enlightened enough to understand that the master can take a real and intelligent interest in planning and arranging, and in watching the working out in detail. His small-minded vanity can only see in all this a distrust in his own powers and an intentional slight cast on his ability, whereas no such idea had ever entered the master's mind.

Though there are many of this kind of gardener (and with their employers, if they have the patience to retain them in their service, I sincerely condole), there are happily many of a widely-different nature, whose minds are both supple and elastic and intelligently receptive, who are eager to learn and to try what has not yet come within the range of their experience, who show a cheerful readiness to receive a fresh range of ideas, and a willing alacrity in doing their best to work them out. Such a servant as this warms his master's heart, and it would do him good to hear, as I have many times heard, the terms in which the master speaks of him. For just as the educated man feels contempt for the vulgar pretension that goes with any exhibition of ignorant vanity, so the evidence of the higher qualities commands his respect and warm appreciation. Among the gardeners I have known, five such men come vividly to my recollection – good men all, with a true love of flowers, and its reflection of happiness written on their kindly faces.

But then, on the other hand, frequent causes of irritation arise between master and man from the master's ignorance and unreasonable demands. For much as the love of gardening has grown of late, there are many owners who have no knowledge of it whatever. I have more than once had visitors who complained of their gardeners, as I thought quite unreasonably, on their own showing. For it is not enough to secure the services of a thoroughly able man, and to pay good wages, and to provide every sort of appliance, if there is no reasonable knowledge of what it is right and just to expect. I have known a lady, after paying a round of visits in great houses, complain of her gardener. She had seen at one place remarkably fine forced strawberries, at another some phenomenal frame Violets, and at a third immense Malmaison Carnations; whereas her own gardener did not excel in any of these, though she admitted that he was admirable for Grapes and Chrysanthemums. 'If the others could do all these things to perfection,' she argued, 'why could not he do them?' She expected her gardener to do equally well all that she had seen best done in the other big places. It was in vain that I pleaded in defence of her man that all gardeners were human creatures, and that it was in the nature of such creatures to have individual aptitudes and special preferences, and that it was to be expected that each man should excel in one thing, or one thing at a time, and so on; but it was of no use, and she would not accept any excuse or explanation.

I remember another example of a visitor who had a rather large place, and a gardener who had as good a knowledge of hardy plants as one could expect. My visitor had lately got the idea that he liked hardy flowers, though he had scarcely thrown off the influence of some earlier heresy which taught that they were more or less contemptible – the sort of thing for cottage gardens; still, as they were now in fashion, he thought he had better have them. We were passing along my flower border, just then in one of its best moods of summer beauty, and when its main occupants, three years planted, had come to their full strength, when, speaking of a large flower border he had lately had made, he said, 'I told my fellow last autumn to get anything he liked, and yet it is perfectly wretched. It is not as if I wanted anything out of the way; I only want a lot of common things like that,' waving a hand airily at my precious border, while scarcely taking the trouble to look at it.

And I have had another visitor of about the same degree of appreciative insight, who, contemplating some cherished garden picture, the consummation of some long-hoped-for wish, the crowning joy of years of labour, said, 'Now look at that; it is just right, and yet it is quite simple – there is absolutely nothing in it; now, why can't my man give me that?'

I am far from wishing to disparage or undervalue the services of the honest gardener, but I think that on this point there ought to be the clearest understanding; that the master must not expect from the gardener accomplishments that he has no means of acquiring, and that the gardener must not assume that his knowledge covers all that can come within the scope of the widest and best practice of his craft. There are branches of education entirely out of his reach that can be brought to bear upon garden planning and arrangement down to the very least detail. What the educated employer who has studied the higher forms of gardening can do or criticise, he cannot be expected to do or understand; it is in itself almost the work of a lifetime, and only attainable, like success in any other fine art, by persons of, firstly, special temperament and aptitude; and, secondly, by their unwearied study and closest application.

But the result of knowledge so gained shows itself throughout the garden. It may be in so simple a thing as the placing of a group of plants. They can be so placed by the hand that knows, that the group is in perfect drawing in relation to what is near; while by the ordinary gardener they would be so planted that they look absurd, or unmeaning, or in some way awkward and unsightly. It is not enough to cultivate plants well; they must also be used well. The servant may set up the canvas and grind the colours, and even set the palette, but the master alone can paint the picture. It is just the careful and thoughtful exercise of the higher qualities that makes a garden interesting, and their absence that leaves it blank, and dull, and lifeless. I am heartily in sympathy with the feeling described in these words in a friend's letter, 'I think there are few things so interesting as to see in what way a person, whose perceptions you think fine and worthy of study, will give them expression in a garden.'

THE STORY OF PENGUIN CLASSICS

Before 1946 ...'Classics' are mainly the domain of academics and students, without readable editions for everyone else. This all changes when a little-known classicist, E. V. Rieu, presents Penguin founder Allen Lane with the translation of Homer's Odyssey that he has been working on and reading to his wife Nelly in his spare time.

1946 The Odyssey becomes the first Penguin Classic published, and promptly sells three million copies. Suddenly, classic books are no longer for the privileged few.

1950s Rieu, now series editor, turns to professional writers for the best modern, readable translations, including Dorothy L. Sayers's *Inferno* and Robert Graves's *The Twelve Caesars*, which revives the salacious original.

1960s 1961 sees the arrival of the Penguin Modern Classics, showcasing the best twentieth-century writers from around the world. Rieu retires in 1964, hailing the Penguin Classics list as 'the greatest educative force of the 20th century'.

1970s A new generation of translators arrives to swell the Penguin Classics ranks, and the list grows to encompass more philosophy, religion, science, history and politics.

1980s The Penguin American Library joins the Classics stable, with titles such as *The Last of the Mohicans* safeguarded. Penguin Classics now offers the most comprehensive library of world literature available.

1990s Penguin Popular Classics are launched, offering readers budget editions of the greatest works of literature. Penguin Audiobooks brings the classics to a listening audience for the first time, and in 1999 the launch of the Penguin Classics website takes them online to an ever larger global readership.

The 21st Century Penguin Classics are rejacketed for the first time in nearly twenty years. This world famous series now consists of more than 1,300 titles, making the widest range of the best books ever written available to millions – and constantly redefining the meaning of what makes a 'classic'.

The Odyssey continues ...

The best books ever written

PENGUIN (🐧) CLASSICS

SINCE 1946

Find out more at www.penguinclassics.com